SLEEPY HOLLOW

A full-length musical
Book by Judy Freed
Music by Elizabeth Doyle
Lyrics by Owen Kalt

www.youthplays.com
info@youthplays.com
424-703-5315

CAST OF CHARACTERS

BROM BONES, the brawny village blacksmith. 20s. Is desperately in love with Katrina Van Tassel, but becomes tongue-tied in her presence. The actor playing Brom doubles as the Headless Horseman. Bass/baritone.

KATRINA VAN TASSEL, the wealthiest, best-educated young woman in Sleepy Hollow. Early 20s. Recently orphaned. Wants to carry out her father's plans to improve the town, but fears she is not capable of doing so alone. Mezzo/soprano.

ICHABOD CRANE, the handsome, poetry-quoting new schoolmaster. 30s. Loathes teaching. Would do and say anything to become rich. Acts considerate and charming when it suits his purpose. A skillful manipulator. Baritone/tenor.

WANDA VAN TASSEL, Katrina's younger cousin. Early/mid-teens. New in town. Wants to be noticed, but tends to alienate people by spouting too many morbid words of wisdom. Mezzo.

HELGA VAN TASSEL, Katrina's aunt. 30s or older. A well-meaning but easily flustered widow. Came to Sleepy Hollow after Katrina's father died to help her settle his affairs. Alto/mezzo.

The Sleepy Hollow Boys (Mischief-makers):

PETE, Mid/late teens. Tenor.

ZEKE, Mid/late teens. High baritone.

MUTTON, Mid/late teens. Bass.

The Townspeople:

CHRIS VAN BRUNDT: Low baritone.

ANNA VAN BRUNDT: Alto.

SOFIE DUTCHER: Soprano.

TIME AND PLACE

The early 1800s. Sleepy Hollow, a Dutch-American village in rural New York State.

SETTING

The Forest. The setting is sparse and open with perhaps a stump or two and possibly the remains of a campfire. Shadows loom ominously.

NOTES

The Townspeople and the Sleepy Hollow Boys double as Forest Voices.

Townspeople can double as instrumentalists.

The cast of 5 women and 6 men can be expanded by adding Townspeople and Schoolchildren to the chorus.

ACKNOWLEDGEMENT

The title page of all programs must contain the following credit: "*Sleepy Hollow* was developed at Theatre Building Chicago and the ASCAP/Disney Musical Theatre Workshop. Special thanks to Scott Sandoe for his creative contributions."

PRODUCTION NOTES

Ambiguities

Did the Headless Horseman get Ichabod Crane, or was Ichabod merely scared out of town? Is there really a Headless Horseman in the forest or not? In keeping with the spirit of Washington Irving's story, the authors have left these questions open to interpretation. There are several places where your production can choose which way to lean:

Act I, Scene 2 (page 25): The strange cry in the forest could come from a mysterious offstage creature...or it could be produced surreptitiously onstage by one of the Sleepy Hollow Boys.

Act I, Scene 4 (page 37): The voices Ichabod hears in the forest could be ghosts and demons...or Ichabod's subconscious fears.

Act I, Scene 6 (page 48): When Wanda enters the forest, she might be chased by the Headless Horseman...or someone might play a prank on her.

Act II, Scene 2 (page 64): The rustling in the bushes might simply be a bat...or there might be a mysterious figure lurking in the underbrush.

Act II, Scene 6 (pages 81-83): Ichabod might be chased by the Headless Horseman and a horde of demons...or by Katrina, Brom, and everyone else in town. Previous productions have used a variety of special effects for the chase scene, including puppetry, video, slide projections, shadow play, creative costuming, strobe lighting and movable set pieces.

Enlarging the Cast

Productions that wish to use a larger cast can add Townspeople and Schoolchildren to the chorus. Additional cast members can sing in "Great Day in the Morning," "Forest Song, Part 1," "Forest Song, Part 2," "The Legend," "Forest Song Part 3/Forest Chase" and the optional bows music ("Great Day in the Morning – Second Act Finale Reprise"). All additional cast members can be part of the dance in "Scare Your Partner." Additional Townspeople can sing in "Mister Fancy Pants."

One-Act Version

The show can be reduced to a one-act that runs about 60 minutes. Musical cuts include omitting "The Forest Song – Intro," "*Sleepy Hollow* Overture" and "Great Day in the Morning (Brom's Reprise);" cutting measures 20-44 of "Mister Fancy Pants," and eliminating "Second Act Opener (Minor Great Day & Welcome)" and "Helga's Menu." The Sleepy Hollow Boys' portion of "Welcome to Sleepy Hollow – End of Act One" is omitted to eliminate the act break.

MUSICAL NUMBERS

ACT I

The Forest Song – Intro: Forest Voices

Sleepy Hollow **Overture:** Instrumental

Welcome to Sleepy Hollow (*Sleepy Hollow* **Opening Part One):** Pete, Zeke, Mutton

Great Day in the Morning (*Sleepy Hollow* **Opening Part Two):** Brom, Katrina, Ensemble *(minus Ichabod)*

Great Day in the Morning (Brom's Reprise): Brom

Horseman Motive (Act I – Scene 2): Instrumental

What's a Girl Got To Do?: Wanda

Act I Scene Change 2 to 3: Instrumental

Nurturing Fertile Young Minds: Ichabod, Katrina

The Forest Song – Part 1: Ichabod, Forest Voices

I'm Not Afraid: Ichabod, Forest Voices

Mr. Fancy Pants: Brom, Chris, Ensemble *(minus Ichabod, Katrina and Wanda)*

*Sleepy Hollow***: Act I Scene Change 5 to 6:** Instrumental

What's a Girl Got To Do? Reprise: Wanda

With Him: Katrina

Welcome to Sleepy Hollow (*Sleepy Hollow* **End of Act I):** Wanda, Helga, Katrina, Brom, Ichabod, Pete, Zeke, Mutton

ACT II

Second Act Opener (Minor Great Day & Welcome): Instrumental

Scare Your Partner: Pete, Zeke, Mutton

The Forest Song – Part 2: Ichabod, Forest Voices

I'm Not Afraid – Part 2: Ichabod, Forest Voices

Act II Scene Change 2 to 3: Instrumental

Helga's Menu: Helga

With Him (Act II Scene 3 to 4): Instrumental

I Know You By Heart: Brom

I Know You By Heart (Continued – Duet): Katrina and Brom

The Legend: Brom, Katrina, Ensemble

The Forest Song – Part 3: Ichabod, Forest Voices/Ensemble

I'm Not Afraid – Part 3: Ichabod, Forest Voices/Ensemble

The Forest Chase: Ichabod, Forest Voices/Ensemble

Welcome to Sleepy Hollow (Act II Finale Reprise): Pete, Zeke, Mutton

OPTIONAL BOWS MUSIC

Great Day in the Morning (Act II Finale Reprise): Ensemble

ACT I

OPTIONAL PRE-OVERTURE MUSIC: The Forest Song – Intro

(This can be used to set the mood in the theater before the overture begins. Repeat as desired.)

MUSIC: Overture

PROLOGUE

(The OVERTURE ends. Lights up on a clearing in the woods. FOREST VOICES hoot like an owl, bay like a wolf, chatter like a raccoon, and make other foreboding animal noises. MUSIC up. The Sleepy Hollow Boys – ZEKE, PETE and MUTTON – enter. They perform some sort of shtick during their entrance: perhaps they enter walking backwards from different corners of the stage, bump into each other center stage, smile, then begin singing to the audience.)

Welcome to Sleepy Hollow (*Sleepy Hollow* Opening Part One)

(If "THE FOREST SONG - INTRO" has been performed, begin at measure 5. If "THE FOREST SONG - INTRO" has not been performed, begin at measure 1 and include foreboding noises from offstage voices.)

MUTTON: WELCOME TO OUR COZY LITTLE TOWN.

SLEEPY HOLLOW BOYS: YOU'LL BE VERY HAPPY HERE IN SLEEPY HOLLOW.
YOU'LL BE SAFE AND SOUND; THIS IS A PEACEFUL ADDRESS –

MUTTON: WELL, MORE OR LESS.

ZEKE: DON'T BELIEVE THE TALK YOU'LL HEAR IN TOWN;

MUTTON & PETE: EV'RYTHING IS PERFECT HERE IN...

MUTTON, PETE & ZEKE: SLEEPY HOLLOW.

SLEEPY HOLLOW BOYS: BUT YOU MIGHT DO ONE SMALL THING BEFORE YOU RELAX— START MAKING TRACKS!

PETE: OUR TOWN'S A CHEERY LITTLE CHARMER WHERE THE WIFE OF EV'RY FARMER GROWS POSIES IN HER FAV'RITE FLOWER BED.

ZEKE: ONCE YOU GET A CHEST FULL OF THAT AIR SO SWEET AND RESTFUL

MUTTON: YOU'LL HARDLY EVEN MIND THE WALKING DEAD.

PETE: THIS IS JUST AN ORDINARY PLACE. NOTHING TOO EXCITING HERE...

SLEEPY HOLLOW BOYS: IN CREEPY-EEPY, EEPY SLEEPY HOLLOW. THIS IS JUST AN AV'RAGE LITTLE TOWN WITH A SCHOOL— AND GRUESOME GHOUL.

ZEKE: HE WILL STEAL A THING YOU CAN'T REPLACE;

SLEEPY HOLLOW BOYS: HE'S COLLECTING HUMAN HEADS FROM SLEEPY HOLLOW. IF YOU MEET HIM YOU'LL STILL BE THE SAME OVERALL—

ZEKE: JUST NOT AS TALL.

PETE: WE DON'T WANT OUR WORDS TO CAUSE A SLEEPLESS NIGHT FOR YOU;

MUTTON: WE DON'T THINK THAT YOU WILL MEET A HORRIFYING FATE,

ZEKE: BUT IF YOU DON'T WANT TO HAVE YOUR BODY TORN IN TWO

SLEEPY HOLLOW BOYS: THEN PAY HEED TO THE MATTERS WE RELATE:

> (As ICHABOD, KATRINA and BROM are described, spotlights come up on each in a separate area of the stage. The Sleepy Hollow Boys may start moving set pieces here to begin the transition from the Forest to the Town Square. Actors playing Townspeople/Voices can help with the scene change.)

MUTTON: COME AND MEET THE PEOPLE IN OUR TALE:

SLEEPY HOLLOW BOYS: SHE'S THE RICHEST LADY HERE IN SLEEPY HOLLOW.
HE'S THE LOCAL BLACKSMITH AND HE LOVES HER, ALTHOUGH—
SHE DOESN'T KNOW.

PETE: SEE THAT MAN WHO'S COMING UP THE TRAIL;

SLEEPY HOLLOW BOYS: HE'LL BE OUR NEW TEACHER HERE IN SLEEPY HOLLOW.
LITTLE DO THESE PEOPLE KNOW THE MOMENTS OF DREAD
THAT LIE AHEAD.

PETE: A head?

ZEKE: (Putting his hands around his throat to indicate strangling:) Get it? A head?

> (The Sleepy Hollow Boys laugh ominously.)

SLEEPY HOLLOW BOYS: SLEEPY HOLLOW, SLEEPY HOLLOW, SLEEPY HOLLOW, SLEEPY HOLLOW!

WELCOME TO OUR COZY LITTLE TOWN...

(There is a bloodcurdling SCREAM from offstage.)

WANDA (O.S.): *(Screaming as if in pain:)* Aaaaahhhhhhh!

(We hear the SOUND of a HORSE WHINNYING. All on stage look up at the sounds of the scream and the horse.)

SLEEPY HOLLOW BOYS: YOU'RE ON YOUR OWN!

(Blackout. In the darkness, we hear the SOUND of Brom HAMMERING RHYTHMICALLY at his anvil. MUSIC up.)

SCENE 1

(The Town Square. Lights up on Brom hammering at his anvil. He is fashioning the blade of a shovel. He stops and wipes his brow.)

Great Day in the Morning (*Sleepy Hollow* Opening Part Two)

BROM: TODAY I WILL SPEAK TO THE WOMAN I LOVE
AND FINALLY ASK HER OUT STROLLING.
THIS IS IT, COME WHAT MAY,
I'LL ASK HER TODAY
IF SHE'LL GO!

(CHRIS enters.)

CHRIS: Morning, Brom! Beautiful day!

BROM: It sure is!

(Brom begins hammering again. As he sings, the TOWNSPEOPLE enter and begin to set up shop for the day. The dark forest has transformed into the cheery town square. The bright autumn morning obliterates the darkness.)

GREAT DAY IN THE MORNING;
I'VE WAITED FOR A CHANCE LIKE THIS.
GREAT DAY IN THE MORNING
TO SPEAK UP WHILE I DARE.
GREAT DAY IN THE MORNING
TO MAYBE SHARE OUR FIRST REAL KISS.
GREAT DAY IN THE MORNING
TO SHOW HER HOW I CARE.

(Katrina enters, accompanied by WANDA and HELGA. Helga and Wanda begin making their rounds of the vendors, buying apples and other produce. Katrina stays off to one side of the stage, and sings to herself.)

ENSEMBLE: GREAT DAY IN THE MORNING

KATRINA: I'M OPENING OUR SCHOOL AT LAST.

ENSEMBLE: GREAT DAY IN THE MORNING

KATRINA: THERE'S JOY THROUGHOUT THE TOWN.

ENSEMBLE: GREAT DAY IN THE MORNING

KATRINA: GREAT CHANGES WILL BE COMING FAST.

ENSEMBLE: GREAT DAY IN THE MORNING

KATRINA: HOPE I DON'T LET FOLKS DOWN.
MY FRIENDS AND MY NEIGHBORS,
THEY'RE COUNTING ON ME.
I'M TERRIBLY NERVOUS
BUT I WON'T LET THEM SEE.

BROM: WHEN WE ARE OUT WALKING, KATRINA AND I,
I'LL FINALLY TELL HER I LOVE HER.
THAT'S WHEN I WILL BECOME
MUCH MORE THAN A CHUM
IN HER EYES.

(Pete, Zeke and Mutton enter.)

ENSEMBLE: GREAT DAY IN THE AUTUMN

SLEEPY HOLLOW BOYS: FOR CATCHING LOTS OF FISH TO FRY.

ENSEMBLE: GREAT DAY IN THE AUTUMN

ALL MEN: TO BRING THE HARVEST IN.

ENSEMBLE: GREAT DAY IN THE AUTUMN

ALL WOMEN: FOR TURNING PUMPKINS INTO PIE.

ENSEMBLE: GREAT DAY IN THE AUTUMN
COME, LET THE DAY BEGIN!

(While Katrina speaks with the vendors, Brom spits on his hand and slicks down his hair.)

CHRIS: Miss Van Tassel, the new books are here. Where do you want me to put them?

KATRINA: Thank you, Chris. You can take the books to the schoolhouse.

ZEKE: Hey, Brom! Give us a hand! We've got a prank to play.

BROM: *(Looking at Katrina:)* Not now, Zeke.

ANNA: *(To Katrina:)* Miss Van Tassel. Do you think the new teacher will need to buy any shoes?

KATRINA: He might, Anna. I'll tell him to see you if he does.

ZEKE: *(To Brom:)* Katrina Van Tassel, eh?

MUTTON: You're not going to court her, are you Brom?

ZEKE: Isn't she a little out of your class?

SOFIE: *(Quietly:)* Miss Van Tassel, about my little boy...

KATRINA: Don't worry, Sofie. I promise I'll find him a nice, warm coat so he can go to school this winter.

PETE: Don't let it stop you, Brom. So you grew up poor, and she's the richest lady in town. You never went to school, and she has a house full of books.

MUTTON: She's wearing a brand new gown, and you've got horse poop on your shirt.

PETE: Don't let that stop you! Don't let it stand in the way of love!

MUTTON: Yeah. What's the worst that could happen?

ZEKE: She could say "no"; she could laugh in your face...

PETE: Look. She's coming this way.

BROM: Go bother someone else. All of you! Go on! Git!

ZEKE: Hey, Brom. You've got something on your teeth.

(The Boys disappear as Katrina approaches Brom.)

KATRINA: Brom! I am so glad to see you! How's the schoolhouse stove? Were you able to repair it?

BROM: *(Trying to clean his teeth without being noticed:)* All fixed.

KATRINA: Is there plenty of wood for the fire?

BROM: All chopped.

KATRINA: Thank goodness. Can you imagine? If Professor Crane had started school tomorrow and he couldn't even warm the schoolhouse? I should have remembered to check that stove weeks ago.

BROM: It's fixed now.

KATRINA: The stove, the wood... What else am I forgetting?

(Katrina paces and fidgets with the lace on her sleeves.)

BROM: Is something the matter?

KATRINA: What do you mean?

BROM: You always...fidget...when you're upset.

(Katrina stops "fidgeting.")

KATRINA: It's nothing, really. I just hope Professor Crane will be happy here.

BROM: Why wouldn't he be happy?

KATRINA: He and Father had so many plans for the town. New hymnals for the church choir, building the town a library... But if anything should go wrong with the school...

BROM: Well, the stove is working fine now. And I patched the hole in the roof.

KATRINA: Are you sure I can't pay you something for your troubles?

BROM: No! The kids in this town deserve a nice place to go to school. I wanted to help.

KATRINA: Thank you, Brom. I don't know what I would have done without you.

BROM: Say, Katrina...I was wondering...

KATRINA: Yes, Brom?

BROM: Well, maybe, if you want... I mean, sometime, uh...if you wouldn't mind...

> *(Brom leans on the shovel suavely. The shovel and Brom crash to the ground. Brom recovers quickly.)*

Your shovel's almost ready!

KATRINA: Thank you for fixing it.

BROM: I'll bring it. To your farm. Tomorrow night.

KATRINA: Whenever it's ready.

BROM: *(Stammering:)* Then maybe...uh...sometime...if it isn't too much trouble...

KATRINA: I'm sorry! I didn't pay you for the shovel! I promise, I'll pay for it whenever you like.

BROM: That's not what I mean!

> *(SOUND of a HORSE NEIGHING.)*

KATRINA: That must be the carriage from Boston. Excuse me. I have to go meet Professor Crane.

BROM: Katrina! Wait!

(Ichabod Crane sweeps into the square, carrying a small bundle of books tied together with twine. He is dressed to the nines, in stark contrast to Brom and the other Men.)

ICHABOD: Ah! What a charming town! *(To Zeke:)* Excuse me, young man. Would you be so kind as to carry these books?

(Zeke takes the books from Ichabod.)

KATRINA: Professor Crane?

ICHABOD: I am he.

KATRINA: I'm Katrina Van Tassel.

ICHABOD: Ah, Lucas Van Tassel's daughter.

KATRINA: I hope you had a pleasant journey from Boston.

ICHABOD: Indeed. As the poet said, "There is a harmony in autumn, and a luster in its sky..."

KATRINA: You've read Shelley?

ICHABOD: Shelley, Shakespeare, Keats...

KATRINA: I love Shelley.

BROM: *(To impress Katrina:)* I can carry my anvil clear across the town square!

PETE: A dollar says you can't.

BROM: Just watch!

(Brom makes a great show of his physical warm-up. Pete, Zeke and Mutton egg him on.)

KATRINA: This is my Aunt Helga and my cousin Wanda. They're visiting from Pennsylvania.

ICHABOD: Visitors. *(To Wanda:)* Does this mean I won't see your smiling face in my classroom?

WANDA: Oh, I'll be there. I wouldn't miss school for the world!

BROM: *(Lifting the anvil:)* Here goes!

(Brom staggers toward Katrina with the anvil as Helga gives Ichabod two strange-looking objects.)

HELGA: I made you a gift, Professor Crane. It's a pair of socks. I knitted them myself!

ICHABOD: How kind of you!

HELGA: They might be a little bit lumpy.

MUTTON: Miss Van Tassel! Look what Brom can do!

ZEKE: Hey Brom, catch!

(Zeke hurls Ichabod's books into the air. Without thinking, Brom hoists the anvil into the arms of Ichabod and catches the books. Ichabod implodes under the weight, or perhaps the anvil falls on his foot.)

KATRINA: Brom!

BROM: Whoa! Sorry there, Professor Crane!

(Brom pulls the anvil off Ichabod and hurls it back at the Boys, who wrestle it back into its customary position.)

KATRINA: Are you all right, Professor?

BROM: Let me help you up.

KATRINA: Shall I call the doctor?

ICHABOD: Not at all. Any wounds are purely superficial. Just tell me where I might find your father, and I shall be on my way.

BROM: Her father?

KATRINA: Professor, didn't you get my letter? My father passed away in June.

ICHABOD: He what?

KATRINA: Don't worry. I'll take care of everything the way you and Father planned. The schoolhouse is ready. The children will be there tomorrow morning at eight o'clock. And please, would you be my guest for supper tomorrow evening?

ICHABOD: Very well. Supper.

HELGA: Tomorrow evening? That doesn't give me much time. I'll have to polish the silver, and wash the walls...

KATRINA: Aunt Helga, why don't you and Wanda take Professor Crane to the inn? *(To Ichabod:)* They've prepared a lovely room for you. Just as Father promised.

WANDA: But make sure you don't use the outhouse after dark.

HELGA: Wanda!

WANDA: A bear might attack you, and rip your head right off! Use the chamber pot instead.

(Ichabod, Helga and Wanda exit.)

BROM: Katrina!

KATRINA: Yes, Brom?

BROM: I... Tomorrow I'll bring you the shovel.

KATRINA: All right. Tomorrow!

(Katrina exits. Left alone on stage, Brom whacks his anvil angrily.)

BROM: Stupid! Stupid! Stupid! Stupid!

(MUSIC up.)

Great Day in the Morning (Brom's Reprise)

BROM: THAT WENT REALLY SMOOTHLY.
MY STAMMER WAS MY VERY BEST.
AND THEN WHEN I DROPPED THINGS,
I'M SURE SHE WAS IMPRESSED.
I'M JUST A BIG BUMPKIN;
I'M NEVER GONNA GET THIS RIGHT.
BUT SHE IS SO SPLENDID...
I'LL TRY TOMORROW NIGHT!

(The Sleepy Hollow Boys enter to change the set.)

SCENE 2

(The Schoolhouse. Ichabod stands at the front of the classroom, ruler in hand. Mutton sleeps peacefully at his desk; Zeke threads a pencil through Mutton's hair. Wanda listens intently.)

ICHABOD: Well. Your parents have done an abysmal job of teaching you grammar. Let's see how little you know of mathematics. You there. What's-your-name.

PETE: Pete.

ICHABOD: Calculate the following sum: one hundred forty-two, minus one hundred thirty-nine, times twelve!

PETE: *(Calculating nervously:)* Thirty-six?

ICHABOD: Now express the solution in Roman numerals.

PETE: I dunno, Professor Crane...

ICHABOD: Stupid fool!

(Ichabod raps Pete on the knuckles.)

PETE: Ow!

WANDA: Professor Crane?

ICHABOD: Yes, Wanda?

WANDA: If you like, I can tell the class about all the ways the Romans used to torture their prisoners!

ICHABOD: The subject is mathematics, not history!

MUTTON: *(Yawning blissfully:)* Aaaahhh!

(The pencil falls out of Mutton's hair.)

ICHABOD: *(To Mutton:)* You there! What are first eight digits of the ratio equaling the circumference of a circle divided by its diameter!

MUTTON: What's the question?

(Ichabod slams Mutton's desk with his ruler.)

ICHABOD: I said, what are the first eight digits of the ratio known as "pi"?

ZEKE: Sure, Professor! I'll have some pie!

(Ichabod whacks Zeke.)

Ow!

ICHABOD: Are you mocking me?

ZEKE: No, Sir!

ICHABOD: Are you contradicting me?

ZEKE: No, Sir!

ICHABOD: You shall all write one hundred times, "I will pay attention in class."

(Wanda and the Boys take out their writing tablets.)

(To himself:) Ignorant guttersnipes!   Miserable little town!   I deserve a better life than this!

(The Boys play a prank on Ichabod such as shooting him in the back with spitballs or wads of paper, or startling him by all dropping their books at the same time.   Ichabod reacts.   Pete, Zeke and Mutton dissolve into laughter.)

I demand that whichever of you rapscallions is responsible for this come forward and accept the thrashing you so richly deserve.

(Pause. No one moves.)

WANDA: Professor Crane, the best way to make someone confess to a crime is to —

(Pete steps on Wanda's foot, cutting her off.)

WANDA: Ow!

ICHABOD: Very well then. If no one will confess, you will *all* receive a sound thrashing. You there. Mutton. You will accompany me to the woodshed first, followed by what-are-your-names. Zeke and Pete.

(A STRANGE CRY is heard from offstage. It could be a cat...or it could be something far more sinister.)

MUSIC: Horseman Motive (Act I - Scene 2)

What was that?

MUTTON: Something's in the forest!

ICHABOD: *(Whacking Mutton:)* I know it's in the forest, you idiot! What is it?

PETE: Strange things happen in the forest all the time.

ZEKE: Like noises.

MUTTON: And voices.

PETE: And sometimes people disappear.

ICHABOD: *(Concerned:)* Disappear?

WANDA: *(Knowingly:)* What is it? Witches? Werewolves?

PETE: A ghost.

MUTTON: The walking dead.

WANDA: *(Knowingly:)* Ahhhhh!

ICHABOD: What sort of...ghost?

PETE: During the War for Independence, a man was beheaded in the forest.

ZEKE: Old Van *(Rhymes with "knew":)* Brugh.

PETE: Accused of treason, but he swore he was innocent 'til the very end.

MUTTON: They say he haunts the forest on a big black horse.

PETE: They say he carries his head under his arm.

ICHABOD: His head?

PETE: He's waiting for the moment he can take his revenge!

ICHABOD: *(To himself:)* Oh, dear.

WANDA: Are you sure it's a ghost?

PETE: It's a ghost.

WANDA: Because demons can take their heads off, too. Back home in Pennsylvania I heard about a demon that—

ICHABOD: *(Cutting off Wanda:)* Silence! Educated people do not believe in ghosts and spirits! I forbid you to mention such superstitious hogwash again. Am I clear?

PETE: Yes, Sir.

MUTTON: Yes, Sir.

ZEKE: Sure are, Professor Crane.

(The STRANGE CRY is heard again. Ichabod starts.)

MUSIC: Horseman Motive (Act I - Scene 2)

ICHABOD: *(Composing himself:)* Well! I have a dinner engagement this evening. In the spirit of good fellowship, I shall postpone your punishment until tomorrow. Class is dismissed!

(Ichabod exits grandly.)

WANDA: You know, it might even be a vampire! Vampires can do all sorts of transformations. They—

PETE: *(Cutting off Wanda:)* Go home, Wanda.

WANDA: I can stay and talk.

ZEKE: It's going to be dark soon.

PETE: Your cousin Katrina's house is on the other side of the forest.

MUTTON: If you don't leave now, you might run into the ghost!

WANDA: That's okay. I know seven different ways to repel a ghost. You can carry iron, or salt, or cross over the water —

BOYS: *(Cutting Wanda off:)* Go home, Wanda!

(The Sleepy Hollow Boys exit.)

WANDA: No one in this town wants to talk about anything!

(MUSIC up.)

What's A Girl Got To Do?

WHAT'S A GIRL GOT TO DO TO GET FOLKS TO SIT FOR A
CHAT?
I TALK ABOUT SOMETHING FUN
AND THEY LEAVE BEFORE I'M DONE.
HOW COME THEY NEVER WANT TO JUST CHEW THE
FAT?
I COULD GIVE A LECTURE ABOUT WHEN TO HUNT FOR
SNAKES
AND WHERE YOU OUGHT TO LOOK TO FIND A BAT.
I COULD TEACH FOLKS HOW TO TELL A MUSHROOM
FROM A TOADSTOOL
AND WHY IT'S CALLED A "ROUNDWORM" THOUGH IT'S
FLAT.
I DON'T SEE HOW FOLKS COULD GET A BIGGER THRILL
THAN THAT!

WHAT'S A GIRL GOT TO DO TO GET FOLKS TO LEND
HER AN EAR?
I TRY TO BE SO NICE
BY GIVING FOLKS ADVICE,
SO WHY WHEN I SAY "HI" DO THEY DISAPPEAR?
I COULD ANSWER QUESTIONS ABOUT HOW TO SCARE
A GHOST:
YOU WHISTLE WHILE YOU'RE TURNING ROUND AND
ROUND AND ROUND AND ROUND.
I COULD TELL THEM HOW TO RID THE TOWN OF EVIL
SPIRITS
BY SPRINK'LING DEAD MEN'S ASHES ON THE GROUND.
THEN THESE FOLKS WOULD SEE THAT I'M A JOY TO
HAVE AROUND!
WHAT'S A GIRL GOT TO DO TO FINALLY MAKE HERSELF
HEARD?
WHAT'S A GIRL GOT TO DO?
I REALLY WISH I KNEW
HOW TO MAKE THESE PEOPLE HANG ON MY EV'RY
WORD.
HOW CAN I MAKE THEM HANG ON MY EV'RY WORD?

(Segue to Scene 3.)

SCENE CHANGE MUSIC: Act I Scene Change 2 to 3

SCENE 3

(The Van Tassel Home. Brom paces back and forth outside the front door, gesturing with a large shovel as he speaks.)

BROM: *(To himself:)* Pull yourself together, Brom. Just talk to her! "Hello, Katrina! I brought your shovel. Do you want to go for a walk tomorrow?" That's all.

(Brom knocks on the door.)

"Hello, Katrina. I brought your shovel."

(He holds out the shovel as Helga answers the door.)

HELGA: Mr. Bones! You brought the shovel! Thank you.

(Helga takes the shovel and shuts the door in Brom's face. Brom knocks again.)

Hello?

BROM: I want to come in.

HELGA: Of course. I'm sorry. Come in! Come in!

(Lights up in the house as Brom enters, revealing Katrina serving tea to Ichabod.)

ICHABOD: The silver work on your tea set is simply stunning.

KATRINA: Thank you.

ICHABOD: Your tea set *is* silver, is it not?

(Katrina is about to answer "Yes" as Brom enters.)

BROM: "Hello Katrina, I—"

HELGA: *(Shrieking:)* Stop!

(Brom freezes in his tracks.)

Mr. Bones! You're tracking mud on Katrina's beautiful carpet!

BROM: I'll take off my boots.

(Brom takes off his boots.)

KATRINA: Hello, Brom.

(Brom opens his mouth to reply, but Helga cuts him off before he can say a word.)

HELGA: *(Cutting Brom off:)* Mr. Bones came all the way from town with your new shovel.

KATRINA: Thank you, Brom.

HELGA: We owe him some apple brown betty!

(Wanda bursts in:)

WANDA: I just remembered! What we were talking about over dinner. It's called a reflex! That's why the chicken can run around after you cut its head off!

KATRINA: Wanda!

WANDA: Even when the blood is spurting out of its neck —

HELGA: Wanda! Help me in the kitchen! We need apple brown betty, right away!

(Helga and Wanda exit.)

KATRINA: Professor Crane, I am so sorry. *(To Brom:)* Brom, please, join us. I was just telling Professor Crane how much we need his advice about choosing books for the library. *(To Ichabod:)* History, for example. Which history books would you recommend?

ICHABOD: Well, Mr. Robertson's *History of England* contains a fascinating account of the War of the Roses. Mr. Bones, are you an aficionado of English history?

BROM: *(Thinking quickly:)* The English invented the forge.

ICHABOD: I'm intrigued. Tell me more.

BROM: There isn't any more.

KATRINA: I'm also hoping Professor Crane will help us choose new hymnals for the church choir. He's quite a fine musician.

ICHABOD: I hate to trumpet my own accomplishments...but I play both the piano and the organ. I received my instruction from a grandson of Johann Sebastian Bach.

(There's a CRASH in the kitchen.)

HELGA (O.S.): Oh, no!

KATRINA: Excuse me. I think Aunt Helga needs help in the kitchen.

(Katrina exits.)

BROM: Sorry about yesterday, Professor.

ICHABOD: Not at all. Not at all. Would you care for a cup of tea?

BROM: No, thanks. But I would like to have some time alone with Miss Van Tassel.

ICHABOD: Alone?

BROM: Hope you don't mind. There's something I need to ask her.

ICHABOD: Is your question of a personal nature?

BROM: Well...yes.

(Katrina enters.)

KATRINA: I'm sorry. Where were we?

ICHABOD: I believe we were discussing the library. Miss Van Tassel, perhaps I could assist you in choosing some volumes of poetry.

KATRINA: I love poetry.

ICHABOD: "If I could write the beauty of your eyes..."

KATRINA: That's Shakespeare, isn't it?

ICHABOD: "See! how she leans her cheek upon her hand:
O! that I were a glove upon that hand,
That I might touch that cheek!"

BROM: Hey!

ICHABOD: *(Taking Katrina's hand:)* "It is love's artillery
Which here contracts itself and comes to lie
Close couched in your white bosom."

BROM: You little snake!

KATRINA: Brom!

BROM: I ought to knock your block off!

KATRINA: What's gotten into you?

BROM: Come on. Step outside.

KATRINA: He'll do nothing of the sort!

ICHABOD: Now, now, my dear. Not everyone appreciates poetry as much as you and I.

BROM: Why, you—

KATRINA: Stop it, Brom! Stop it right now!

(Katrina steps between Ichabod and Brom:)

I think you had better say goodnight, Brom.

BROM: But, Katrina—

KATRINA: Goodnight, Brom.

(Brom starts to leave.)

ICHABOD: Good evening, Mr. Bones! Don't forget your boots!

(Brom returns, picks up his boots and exits, boots in hand.)

KATRINA: I am so sorry, Professor Crane!

ICHABOD: Please. Think nothing of it.

KATRINA: I don't know what's gotten into Brom! Or Wanda!

ICHABOD: Your cousin's enthusiasm is quite...refreshing.

KATRINA: And thank you for being so understanding about Aunt Helga's cooking. The roast was a little burnt.

ICHABOD: Not at all. It was delicious. Having Aunt Helga here must be such a comfort to you.

KATRINA: I don't know what I'm going to do without her. When my father died, she and Wanda came here all the way from Pennsylvania.

ICHABOD: And they'll be leaving after the harvest?

KATRINA: They have to go back to their farm before the first snowfall.

ICHABOD: And then you shall be alone.

KATRINA: Yes.

ICHABOD: All alone, with so many responsibilities.

KATRINA: It is a lot to manage. The farm, the school, the library...

ICHABOD: This beautiful home...

KATRINA: Yes.

ICHABOD: If there's anything I can do to help... Perhaps review the plans for the library building? Conduct the church choir?

KATRINA: Professor Crane! That would be wonderful!

ICHABOD: *(About to say something derogatory:)* As for teaching school...

> *(MUSIC up.)*

KATRINA: Of course. Teaching school is the most important thing of all!

Nurturing Fertile Young Minds

I THINK TEACHING'S A GIFT
AND I KNOW YOU'LL UPLIFT
ALL THE CHILDREN WHO LIVE AROUND HERE.
ON THIS GLORIOUS GLOBE,
I DON'T THINK THERE'S A NOBLER CAREER.

ICHABOD: Why, yes!
EV'RY EVENING, I SIT ABOUT AND GET LOST IN
THOUGHT
AS I THINK OF EACH LITTLE ANGEL WHOM I HAVE
TAUGHT;
THEIR EXPRESSIONS OF UTTER DELIGHT
WHEN I TAUGHT THEM TO READ AND TO WRITE.
NOTHING CAN EQUAL THE JOY A MAN FINDS
NURTURING FERTILE YOUNG MINDS.
TOUGH, BUT I LOVE IT.
THANKLESS? WHAT OF IT?
OH, WHAT A MARVELOUS LIFE!
EV'RY CHILD IN CLASS IS SO EAGER, THEY ALL INSIST
THAT I LET THEM STUDY LONG AFTER THEY'VE BEEN
DISMISSED;

AND THEY BEG TO SPEND THREE DAYS A WEEK
TRYING HARD TO BE FLUENT IN GREEK.
NOTHING CAN EQUAL THE JOY A MAN FINDS
NURTURING FERTILE YOUNG MINDS.
OH, HOW THEY CLAMOR:
"PLEASE, TEACH US GRAMMAR."
OH, WHAT A FABULOUS LIFE!

KATRINA: WHEN YOU TEACH THEM TO SPELL,
DO YOU SCOLD THEM OR YELL?

ICHABOD: NO, THERE'S NEVER A NEED TO BE STERN;
AND THERE'S NO NEED TO SPANK
FOR THEY'RE PERFECTLY ANXIOUS TO LEARN.
THOUGH I SOMETIMES HAVE TO GO HUNGRY TO BUY
MORE CHALK,
EV'RY DAY SPENT TEACHING IS WELL WORTH MY
THREE MILE WALK,
JUST TO SEE A BOY BURSTING WITH PRIDE
ON THE DAY HE LEARNS HOW TO DIVIDE.
NOTHING CAN EQUAL THE JOY A MAN FINDS
NURTURING FERTILE YOUNG MINDS.
HELPING TO RAISE THEM,
PAUSING TO PRAISE THEM.

KATRINA: HOPE YOU WON'T MIND IF I GUSH
BUT YOU'RE SO UNSELFISH THAT I CAN'T HELP BUT
APPLAUDING.
I CAN'T HELP ADMIRING;
YOU'RE SO INSPIRING.

ICHABOD: STOP IT, YOU'RE MAKING ME BLUSH!

KATRINA: OH, WHAT A WONDERFUL

ICHABOD: YES, WHAT A FABULOUS

KATRINA & ICHABOD: OH, WHAT A MARVELOUS LIFE!

KATRINA: Professor Crane, I'm so glad you came to Sleepy Hollow!

ICHABOD: Please, call me Ichabod.

(Ichabod is about to take Katrina's hand. Suddenly, an OWL HOOTS. Ichabod freezes.)

What was that?

KATRINA: An owl, I think.

ICHABOD: It sounded like someone screaming.

KATRINA: Sometimes they sound almost human, don't they? Now, about the church choir—

ICHABOD: Perhaps we could discuss the choir tomorrow.

KATRINA: I'm sorry. It's getting late, isn't it?

ICHABOD: I have a long walk ahead of me.

KATRINA: Goodnight, then.

ICHABOD: May I see you again tomorrow?

KATRINA: If you like.

ICHABOD: Wild horses couldn't keep me away.

(He kisses her hand. The OWL HOOTS again.)

KATRINA: Until tomorrow, then.

(Katrina exits. MUSIC up. The cheerful lights of the Van Tassel home dim, and ominous shadows fall across the stage. The Sleepy Hollow Boys enter, grinning, and begin to change the set. Ichabod is plunged into the depths of the forest.)

SCENE 4

(The Forest. VOICES hoot and chatter ominously as Ichabod pulls his coat tighter against the chill. He begins walking through the forest – tentatively at first, then with purpose.)

The Forest Song - Part 1

VOICE: *(Like an owl:)* HOOT, HOOT.

ICHABOD: They do sound almost human...

VOICE: *(Like a crow:)* CAW, CAW. CAW, CAW.

VOICE: *(Like a raccoon:)* CH-CH-CH-CH-CH-CH. CH-CH-CH-CH-CH-CH.

ICHABOD: It certainly is dark...

VOICE 1: *(Whispering:)* DARK...

ICHABOD: But I'm not in any danger.

VOICE 2: *(Whispering:)* DANGER...

ICHABOD: No point in scaring myself to death.

ALL VOICES: *(Quietly, together:)* DEATH...

I'm Not Afraid

ICHABOD: *(Covering his nervousness:)* OH, I'M NOT AFRAID OF THE DARKNESS;
IT'S MERELY THE ABSENCE OF LIGHT.
THE YOKELS MAY BE SUPERSTITIOUS,
BUT I'M A LITTLE TOO BRIGHT.
SO WHERE SHOULD I BE AFRAID?
NOWHERE.
OF WHOM SHOULD I BE AFRAID?
NO ONE.
AND WHEN SHOULD I BE AFRAID?

NEVER.

NOWHERE. NO ONE. NEVER. NOT I!

(The forest is silent as the "HORSEMAN MOTIVE" plays. Glowing eyes appear near Ichabod.)

VOICE: *(Chattering like a raccoon:)* CH-CH-CH-CH-CH-CH! CH-CH-CH-CH-CH-CH!

(Another pair of glowing eyes appears on the other side of Ichabod.)

VOICE: *(Hooting like an owl:)* WHO?

ICHABOD: Oh, dear!

(Ichabod hurries offstage. The MUSIC ends. After a brief pause, the Sleepy Hollow Boys emerge, grinning, and change the set.)

SCENE 5

(The Town Square. Brom works at his anvil as the Townspeople set up shop for the day. The Sleepy Hollow Boys observe.)

SOFIE: Anna! Did you hear what Professor Crane did for Miss Van Tassel?

BROM: Crane!

(He slams metal furiously with his hammer.)

SOFIE: He wrote her a poem. "Your beauty shines brighter than the stars." Isn't that romantic?

BROM: *(Under his breath:)* I'd like to cram those books right down his throat.

CHRIS: Anna, this pumpkin smells like the hind end of a horse.

ANNA: *(Smacking Chris:)* Why don't you ever quote poetry?

SOFIE: Professor Crane has been keeping company with Miss Van Tassel for over a month now. Every time he sees her, he brings her flowers.

(Chris bites into an apple, BELCHES loudly and spits on the ground.)

ANNA: Mind your manners!

SOFIE: The men in this town are simply horrid!

ANNA: No class! No couth!

(MUSIC up.)

SOFIE: You should all be more like Professor Crane.

BROM: Professor Crane?

Mr. Fancy-Pants

WOMEN: HE'S VERY CHARMING AND HE'S FULL OF WIT.

CHRIS: HE'S FULL OF WHAT?

WOMEN: HE'S ALWAYS PERFECTLY WELL-DRESSED.

CHRIS: HE'S A POMPOUS PEACOCK.

WOMEN: YOU NEVER SEE HIM PICK HIS TEETH OR SPIT. COULD ANYBODY FAIL TO BE IMPRESSED?

CHRIS: HE'S A LOUSY SHOW-OFF.

MEN: WE CAN'T STAND MISTER FANCY-PANTS, MISTER KNOW-IT-ALL, MISTER HOITY-TOITY, WE CAN'T STAND MISTER FANCY-PANTS WITH HIS NOSE UP IN THE AIR.

BROM: HOW CAN ALL THE LADIES LIKE THAT PRISSY POWDER PUFF?

CHRIS: EV'RY TIME HE BOWS I'M GONNA KICK HIM IN THE DUFF.

WOMEN: HE IS SUCH A JOY.

CHRIS: HE'S A MAMA'S BOY.

WOMEN: HE'S POLITE AND QUAINT.

MEN: AND YOU MEAN WE AIN'T?

BROM: HE'S NEVER CAUGHT A FISH OR SHOT A DEER.

WOMEN: HE SIPS HIS TEA.

CHRIS: OR PLAYED A PRANK OR BROKE A LIMB.

WOMEN: HE EXTENDS HIS PINKIE.

CHRIS: HE NEVER TAKES A CHEW OR GUZZLES BEER.

MEN: SO, WHAT THE HECK DO WOMEN SEE IN HIM?

WOMEN: DON'T YOU LOVE HIS MANNERS?
WE JUST LOVE MISTER WONDERFUL,
MISTER COURTEOUS,
MISTER "PLEASE AND THANK YOU";
WE ADORE MISTER SENSITIVE,
AND WE WISH YOU WERE LIKE HIM.
MEN AS FINE AS ICHABOD ARE FEW AND FAR
BETWEEN.
HE'S THE ONLY MAN IN TOWN WHOSE FINGERNAILS
ARE CLEAN.
HE IS SO GENTEEL.

BROM: HE'S NO BIG DEAL.

WOMEN: AND HE DOESN'T BURP.

CHRIS: HE IS SUCH A TWERP!

MEN: WE CAN'T STAND MISTER FANCY-PANTS

WOMEN: MISTER WONDERFUL

MEN: MISTER NAMBY-PAMBY.

WOMEN: WE JUST LOVE MISTER ELEGANT.
HE'S A MAN OF TASTE.

CHRIS: HE'S A PANTYWAIST.

WOMEN: HE IS WORLDLY WISE.

MEN: HE'S THE BOOBY PRIZE!

ALL: AND WE KNOW YOU KNOW IT'S TRUE!

(Ichabod enters, carrying his schoolbooks. As usual, he is dressed to the nines.)

ICHABOD: *(Bowing grandly:)* Good morning, ladies!

SOFIE: Morning, Professor Crane!

ANNA: Morning, Professor!

ICHABOD: *(To Sofie:)* Mrs. Dutcher. Has anyone ever told you that you have a voice like a bell?

SOFIE: I do?

ICHABOD: I hope you'll consider joining the church choir. It would be heavenly to hear you singing the solo passage in the Christmas liturgy.

SOFIE: Sure! I'll join the choir!

ICHABOD: *(To Anne:)* And Mrs. Van Brundt. You're looking quite lovely this morning. As the poet says, "She is fair as is the rose in May."

ANNA: *(Nudging Sofie:)* Hear that? It's poetry!

ICHABOD: Good day, ladies.

SOFIE: Good day, Professor.

ANNA: Isn't he charming!

CHRIS: *(Mocking, under his breath:)* "Isn't he charming!"

(The Women exit. Ichabod strolls over to Brom's anvil.)

ICHABOD: Ah, Mr. Bones. Pounding metal into submission so early in the day?

(Brom whacks his anvil, not trusting himself to respond.)

CHRIS: *(To himself:)* Bet he's not so "charming" when the chips are down.

PETE: Hey, Professor Crane!

ICHABOD: Yes?

PETE: That's a mighty nice suit you're wearing.

ICHABOD: Why, thank you.

CHRIS: Yeah. You look real pretty. Maybe you could write a poem about it.

(Brom listens and watches, amused.)

ICHABOD: Gentlemen, I don't mean to be rude, but I'm on my way to the classroom.

PETE: This won't take long, Professor. Just need your help with a science problem.

MUTTON: Yeah. We can't figure out what this thing is.

(Pulling a furry object from his pocket or from behind his back:)

Do you think it's a dead rat, or a dead skunk?

ICHABOD: Oh! Take it away!

(Chris and the Boys taunt Ichabod with the animal carcass.)

CHRIS: What's the matter, Professor? Thought you were an expert in "the local flora and fauna."

ZEKE: Maybe he doesn't like it 'cause it's not wearing a suit.

CHRIS: Now, Zeke. Mind your manners! Careful you don't push the Professor into that horse manure!

(Chris and the Sleepy Hollow Boys are about to push Ichabod into a pile of horse droppings when Brom intervenes.)

BROM: That's enough! Leave the Professor alone! *(Aside, to Chris and the Sleepy Hollow Boys:)* Listen, I don't like him any more than you do. But he's here to teach school. So leave him be.

CHRIS: Mind your manners, Crane. I'll be watching you.

(Chris and the Sleepy Hollow Boys exit.)

BROM: You all right?

ICHABOD: Well. I see you occasionally put your brawn to good use.

BROM: It's not right for them to gang up on a fellow.

ICHABOD: Stirring words, Mr. Bones. Nevertheless, tales of this heroic exploit shall not win you her affections.

BROM: Win what?

ICHABOD: I have the superior intellect, the superior breeding. A lady such as Miss Van Tassel invariably prefers a gentleman such as myself over a common brute like you!

BROM: A brute? Why you...you...

(As Brom prepares to lunge at Ichabod, Katrina enters:)

KATRINA: Ichabod? Brom?

(Brom and Ichabod step back.)

ICHABOD: Katrina. My dearest. Mr. Bones and I, we were just—discussing poetry.

KATRINA: I'm so pleased you two were finally having a talk.

BROM: *(Dryly:)* Professor Crane was doing most of the talking.

ICHABOD: *(To Katrina:)* And Mrs. Dutcher was pleased as punch when I invited her to join the church choir.

KATRINA: I knew she would be. Thank you so much for asking her.

ICHABOD: Well. I'm off to sow the seeds of knowledge! Mustn't keep our eager young scholars waiting!

KATRINA: Ichabod, Aunt Helga wants to know what time you'll be over for supper this evening.

ICHABOD: Dear Aunt Helga. Tell her I shall arrive promptly after choir practice. I hope with all my heart that tonight shall be a memorable evening for you and I.

(Ichabod exits.)

BROM: *(To himself:)* Tonight. *(To Katrina:)* Katrina?

KATRINA: Yes?

BROM: I need to ask you something... Did Shakespeare write poetry?

KATRINA: Yes, he did! William Shakespeare wrote beautiful sonnets.

BROM: I'd like to visit your house sometime. Would that be all right?

KATRINA: Of course, Brom! You're welcome anytime.

(Katrina exits.)

BROM: A common brute, am I? Well, I can learn poetry as well as any man. I know I have a pair of clean shoes somewhere...

(Brom exits.)

SCENE CHANGE MUSIC: Sleepy Hollow: Act I Scene Change 5 to 6

SCENE 6

(The Schoolhouse. Ichabod paces in front of the classroom with his ruler. Wanda frantically tries to get his attention, while Pete passes a note to Mutton and Zeke.)

ICHABOD: If a carriage leaves Plymouth traveling east carrying four kegs of cider weighing twenty pounds each —

WANDA: Professor Crane!

ICHABOD: — and the weight of each keg slows the carriage by one and three-quarter miles an hour, and the horse is capable of pulling an empty carriage at a pace of ten miles an hour for two hours before stopping to rest —

WANDA: Professor Crane!

ICHABOD: — at what point will the driver be forced to change horses? Mutton?

(Mutton reads the note and nods to Pete.)

Mutton?

MUTTON: I don't know, Professor Crane.

(Ichabod raps Mutton on the knuckles.)

Ow!

ICHABOD: Zeke?

ZEKE: Search me.

(Ichabod whacks Zeke:)

Ow!

WANDA: Professor Crane! I know the answer!

ICHABOD: Yes, Wanda.

WANDA: If a carriage leaves Plymouth traveling east, the driver will fall into the ocean and drown! *(Proudly:)* Plymouth is on Plymouth Bay!

ICHABOD: Are you mocking me?

WANDA: No, Sir.

ICHABOD: Are you contradicting me?

WANDA: No, Sir!

ICHABOD: Are you questioning my authority?

WANDA: No, Sir! But Plymouth is on a bay, and—

ICHABOD: I will not be contradicted, you insolent brat!

(Ichabod raises his ruler as if he's about to strike Wanda.)

WANDA: Please don't hit me!

(Ichabod stops himself, and lowers the ruler.)

ICHABOD: Miss Van Tassel. This evening, when I call on your cousin Katrina, I would prefer not to discuss this incident with your mother.

WANDA: Yes, Professor Crane.

ICHABOD: You will not contradict me in the future.

WANDA: No, Professor Crane.

ICHABOD: You will write one hundred times, "I shall keep my opinions to myself."

WANDA: Yes, Professor Crane.

ICHABOD: Class is dismissed.

(Ichabod exits grandly. Wanda begins writing on her tablet.)

WANDA: This isn't fair. Plymouth is on a bay!

MUTTON: Keep your opinions to yourself, Wanda.

PETE: Children should be seen and not heard!

ZEKE: That's something I'd like to see. Wanda, with her mouth shut!

(MUSIC up. Pete, Zeke and Mutton exit, laughing and taunting Wanda.)

What's a Girl Got To Do? Reprise

WANDA: WHAT'S A GIRL GOT TO DO TO MAKE ALL THESE PEOPLE EAT CROW?
THEY TELL ME I SHOULD KEEP MUM,
BUT WHY SHOULD A GIRL PLAY DUMB?
IT'S NOT MY FAULT I KNOW ALL THE THINGS I KNOW.
THEY'D BE AWF'LLY SORRY IF THEY HEARD THAT I GOT SICK
OR MAYBE GOT DEMONICALLY POSSESSED.
MAYBE IF THEY HEARD THAT I WAS CAPTURED BY A PIRATE
WHO KILLED ME WITH A SABER THROUGH MY CHEST

(With great satisfaction:)

THEN THEY ALL WOULD MISS ME AND THEY'D REALLY GET DEPRESSED!
WHAT'S A GIRL GOT TO DO TO KEEP FOLKS FROM WALKING AWAY?
IF A GOBLIN CUT OFF MY HEAD
AND I KEEP TALKING THOUGH I'M DEAD,
THEY'D MAYBE WANT TO HEAR WHAT I HAVE TO SAY.

(Offstage, the FOREST VOICES HOOT and CHATTER.)

WANDA: THEY MIGHT FINALLY WANT TO HEAR WHAT I HAVE TO SAY.

(Wanda strides purposefully offstage.)

SCENE 7

(The Van Tassel Home. Helga bustles about frantically, as Katrina tries to calm her.)

HELGA: Professor Crane will be here any minute. And I haven't had time to pound the dirt out of the carpets! Katrina, where's Wanda?

KATRINA: I don't know. I haven't seen her since this morning.

HELGA: Wanda's not here; the table's not set; I haven't washed the windows...

KATRINA: Ichabod won't care about the windows. Aunt Helga, I think tonight he's going to ask me to marry him.

HELGA: Oh. Goodness. A proposal of marriage!

KATRINA: Yes.

HELGA: If you say "yes" he'll be entitled to everything you own, whether you marry him or not!

KATRINA: I know, Aunt Helga.

HELGA: This is such an important decision! What are you going say?

KATRINA: Well... *(Thinking aloud:)* Father thought quite highly of Ichabod. He and Father had a lengthy correspondence.

HELGA: Your father always hoped you'd marry an educated man.

KATRINA: But Father never actually met Ichabod.

HELGA: No, they never actually met.

KATRINA: He's intelligent. Well mannered. He's doing wonderful things for the town.

HELGA: The ladies think Professor Crane is the best catch in Sleepy Hollow!

KATRINA: But this is all happening so quickly! I've only known him for a few weeks.

HELGA: That's true. Just a few weeks. *(She catches herself:)* I'm not being very helpful, am I?

KATRINA: That's all right.

HELGA: I wish Lucas was here. He would know what to tell you.

KATRINA: I wish Father were here, too.

(Helga pats Katrina on the hand.)

HELGA: I'd better go set the table. *(She stops for a moment:)* Katrina. I think if your father was here, he'd tell you to make whatever decision will make you happy.

(Helga exits. MUSIC up.)

With Him

KATRINA: FOR MANY MONTHS NOW, I HAVE FELT SO LOST.
THE WORLD EXPECTS MUCH MORE THAN I CAN DO.
I LIE AWAKE AT NIGHT FOR HOURS, MAKING PLANS
AND I WONDER IF I'LL EVER SEE THEM THROUGH.
NOW SUDDENLY MY LIFE MAY TAKE A TURN,
AS IF THE WORLD WERE CHANGING ON A WHIM.
I'VE MET THE MOST IMPRESSIVE MAN I'VE EVER KNOWN.
COULD EVERYTHING BE DIFF'RENT NOW WITH HIM?
WITH HIM, WOULD I HAVE SOMEONE HERE BESIDE ME?
WITH HIM, WOULD I NO LONGER FEEL ALONE?
WITH HIM, COULD I HANDLE WHAT FATE HANDS ME?

I HAVE WORRIED SO LONG ABOUT WHAT LIES AHEAD.
WITH HIM, COULD I FACE THE UNKNOWN?
IF I CANNOT SAY "YES" TO HIS PROPOSAL,
I WONDER WHETHER WE'D REMAIN AS FRIENDS.
BUT IF I SAY "YES,"
WOULD I HAVE MAN TO COUNT ON?
WITH HIM, I SEEM TO FEEL SO OPTIMISTIC.
WITH HIM, PERHAPS I'LL STAY THIS WAY FOR GOOD.
WITH HIM, I DO FEEL STRONGER THAN WITHOUT HIM.
I HAVE DREAMED FOR SO LONG ABOUT CHANGING MY
WORLD.
WITH HIM, I THINK MAYBE I COULD.

(SOUND of a KNOCK at the door.)

Just a moment!

(Katrina adjusts her hair and clothing, then opens the door.)

Ichabod?

(Brom stands at the door in his Sunday best. His hair is combed within an inch of its life. His clothes are so well pressed he can barely move. His tight, shiny shoes have never been worn before. He carries a handful of wilted flowers.)

BROM: Flowers!

KATRINA: Brom! Thank you.

BROM: Talk, I have to Katrina.

KATRINA: It's sweet of you to stop by.

BROM: I mean, Katrina, I have to talk.

KATRINA: But I'm expecting Ichabod any minute. Can we talk tomorrow?

BROM: No.

KATRINA: Next week, then?

BROM: I have to talk today.

KATRINA: All right then. What do you want to talk about?

BROM: It's, it's...the way I feel...

(Brom gestures helplessly.)

KATRINA: Please, Brom. I have a very important decision to make.

(Brom gets down on one knee.)

BROM: "I shall compare thee to a summer's hay."

KATRINA: What?

BROM: "Thou art more temperate.   In May thy buds do shake."

KATRINA: I beg your pardon!

BROM: *(Increasingly desperate:)* "Rough wind will make you too short to mate!"

KATRINA: You're making fun of Ichabod!

BROM: No!

KATRINA: Stop it, Brom! He'll be here any minute!

BROM: I am not making fun of him!

KATRINA: I thought I could count on you. I thought you wanted what was best for Sleepy Hollow. But if you want to joke at Ichabod's expense, do it somewhere else.

BROM: "Thy navel is like a round goblet."

KATRINA: Goodbye, Brom!

(Katrina slams the door on Brom, then leans against the door, stunned. Ichabod enters from the garden with a single rose.)

ICHABOD: Katrina, my dearest. This rose is for you.

KATRINA: Ichabod, it's beautiful!

ICHABOD: I've just finished conducting the church choir. I hope it shall not be my last rehearsal. Anna Dutcher so loves to sing...

KATRINA: Your last rehearsal? Why would it be your last rehearsal?

ICHABOD: Katrina, you must be aware of the depth of my feelings for you. And you've given me cause to hope that you share similar feelings in return.

(A KNOCK on the door interrupts Ichabod.)

KATRINA: Excuse me. This won't take a minute.

(Katrina opens the door. It's Brom.)

BROM: Katrina, I didn't mean to—

KATRINA: Go away!

(Katrina slams the door.)

(To Ichabod:) I'm sorry. You were saying?

ICHABOD: You've given me cause to hope that you share similar feelings in return.

(There's another KNOCK on the door. Katrina ignores it.)

If you tell me that you share these feelings, you shall make me the happiest man on earth. But if you do not...

BROM (O.S.): *(Or perhaps we see him through a window:)* Katrina!

ICHABOD: How can I stay in Sleepy Hollow if my heart is broken? The decision is yours. "Bid my heart to stay, and it will stay/To honor thy decree/Or bid it to hasten quite away/And it shall do so...for thee."

(Helga rushes in.)

HELGA: Don't worry! I'll get it!

(Helga opens the door. Brom enters.)

ICHABOD: Katrina Van Tassel, will you marry me?

BROM: Katrina!

KATRINA: Yes, Ichabod, I will marry you.

BROM: But you can't marry Professor Crane!

HELGA: Why not?

BROM: Because...because...

(Wanda bursts into the room. Her clothes are disheveled and torn; there is dirt on her face.)

WANDA: The most amazing thing just happened!

HELGA: Not now, Wanda. Katrina has some wonderful news.

(MUSIC up.)

WANDA: Well, my news is even bigger! I barely escaped with my life!

Welcome to Sleepy Hollow (*Sleepy Hollow* End of Act I)

COME AND HEAR WHAT HAPPENED IN THE WOODS:
I WAS ALMOST MURDERED BY THE HEADLESS
HORSEMAN!
I WAS ON THE FOOTPATH, FEELING DOWN ON MY
LUCK—
AND THEN HE STRUCK!

I COULD HEAR THE HOOF BEATS;
HE WAS GAINING ON ME QUICK.

HELGA: Oh, no!

WANDA: I'M NO GOOD AT RUNNING,
BUT I TRIED MY VERY BEST.

HELGA: And then...?

WANDA: HE WAS GETTING NEAR
SO I PICKED UP A HEAVY STICK
AND THINKING QUICKLY,
I WHACKED HIM IN THE CHEST!
HE FELL OFF HIS HORSE AND I ESCAPED.

ICHABOD: This is not possible!

WANDA: I SHOULD TELL THE TOWN I SAW —

ALL: — THE HEADLESS HORSEMAN.

WANDA: THEY SHOULD HEAR THE DETAILS OF THAT
FEARSOME ATTACK —
'CAUSE HE'LL BE BACK!

ICHABOD: No!
THAT IS NOT WHAT HAPPENED IN THE WOODS...

HELGA: SUCH A THING TO HAPPEN IN THE WOODS...

WANDA: THEY SHOULD HEAR WHAT HAPPENED IN
THE WOODS...

BROM & KATRINA: ARE YOU SURE THAT HAPPENED IN
THE WOODS? HERE IN...

ALL: SLEEPY HOLLOW, SLEEPY HOLLOW, SLEEPY
HOLLOW!

(There is a SCREAM from offstage. Ichabod faints. Brom catches him. Lights fade rapidly on the Van Tassel home.

Suddenly, the Sleepy Hollow Boys jump up to frighten the audience, possibly from positions in the audience seating section. They may wear pumpkin heads or other scary masks. Once the audience knows it's them, the Boys sing.)

SLEEPY HOLLOW BOYS: CHANCES ARE YOUR BACKSIDE IS STARTING TO ACHE,
SO STRETCH YOUR LEGS, TAKE A BREAK,
HAVE A SNACK
AND HEAD ON BACK!

ZEKE: *(To Pete and Mutton:)* Hey, "Head!"

(Pete either hits Zeke in the back of his head, kicks him in the backside, or pushes him back.)

PETE: Back!

(Blackout. End of Act I.)

ACT II

SCENE 1

MUSIC: Second Act Opener (Minor Great Day & Welcome)

(The Town Square. Spotlight up on Wanda, regaling Anna, Chris and Sofie.)

WANDA: So I picked up a branch, and I stabbed him in the chest. I barely escaped with my life! *(Beat.)* If you have any questions, I'd be happy to tell you more.

(MUSIC up as the Townspeople swarm Wanda.)

TOWNSPEOPLE: *(All at once:)* Wanda! How tall was it? How fast did it run? Wanda!

(The Sleepy Hollow Boys enter.)

Scare Your Partner

SLEEPY HOLLOW BOYS: *(To the audience:)* SCARE YOUR PARTNER.
PEOPLE TAKE YOUR PLACES
AND WE'LL PUT YOU THROUGH YOUR PACES; NOW
GET SET TO GO.

(The Sleepy Hollow Boys dance with Wanda and the Townspeople, disrupting Wanda's lecture.)

FLUTTER LIKE A VAMPIRE BAT AND GIVE YOUR GAL A FRIGHT;
THEN YOU SKULK LIKE A WOLF ON THE PROWL;
SWING AND SWAY YOUR PARTNER TO THE LEFT AND TO THE RIGHT;
NOW YOU STARE IN THE AIR AND YOU HOWL.

BITE YOUR GAL UPON THE THROAT, BUT ONLY IF THAT
GAL'S YOUR FIANCÉE;
FORM A RING AND CIRCLE RIGHT — YOU'RE GOING
WRONG, GO BACK THE OTHER WAY.
SCARE YOUR PARTNER.
HOP-STEP TO THE FIDDLE
AS YOU MOVE INTO THE MIDDLE AND THEN BOW
DOWN LOW.

SOFIE: Wanda, how will we protect ourselves?

CHRIS: Let's go kill it!

ANNA: You can't kill it! It's already dead!

WANDA: You need horseshoes. Or bells. Something made of
iron. Iron keeps the spirits away!

*(Mutton sneaks off and hides. Pete and Zeke dance with Wanda
and the Townspeople to distract them.)*

SLEEPY HOLLOW BOYS: MAKE A FACE THAT'S
HORRIBLE ENOUGH TO SCARE YOUR KIN
AND THEN LEAP ALL AROUND LIKE A GOON;
SWIVEL AS YOU'RE DANCING TO THE WICKED VIOLIN;
MOVE YOUR FEET TO THE BEAT OF THE TUNE.
SHUFFLE LIKE A BOGEYMAN, THEN SASHAY DOWN
THE CENTER TWO BY TWO;
BOYS SWING OUT AND GIRLS SWING IN, THEN RISE UP
LIKE A GHOST AND HOLLER —

(Mutton runs through the crowd, possibly in a creepy mask.)

MUTTON: "BOO!"

SLEEPY HOLLOW BOYS: SCARE YOUR PARTNER.
SCARE YOUR PARTNER.
SCARE YOUR PARTNER.

(Shouting:)

Scare your partner!

(Pete, Zeke and Mutton chase Wanda and the Townspeople offstage. The Boys collapse with laughter.)

ZEKE: Did you see how they ran?

MUTTON: Especially Wanda!

PETE: Hey! I've got an idea.

(Brom enters.)

BROM: Afternoon, boys.

MUTTON: Here, Brom! Take a mask!

PETE: Tonight's All Hallow's Eve!

ZEKE: There's gonna be a party!

PETE: We've got mischief to plan!

BROM: Oh, no you don't. Don't you dare ruin Katrina's party.

ZEKE: What's the matter with you?

MUTTON: I know! I know! *(Proud he finally can answer a question:)* He's mad because Katrina's gonna marry the teacher!

PETE: *(Teasing:)* Aw. Poor Brom.

ZEKE: Is your heart breaking?

PETE: Gonna make one last, desperate attempt to get her for yourself?

BROM: *(Defeated:)* No. Professor Crane makes her happy. He's smart. He knows poetry. He's perfect for her.

PETE: He's perfect for her, all right.

ZEKE: Yeah. They both walk around town like they own the place.

BROM: Don't say that about Katrina!

ZEKE: Want to fight about it?

BROM: Yeah. I think I do!

(Pete and Mutton circle as Brom and Zeke prepare for battle. Brom picks up Zeke by the scruff of the neck as Katrina enters.)

KATRINA: Brom! Leave that poor boy alone!

BROM: But he said —

KATRINA: What's gotten into you? It isn't like you to pick a fight.

(Brom puts Zeke down.)

ZEKE: Thanks, Miss Van Tassel.

KATRINA: *(To Zeke:)* Did he hurt you?

ZEKE: Just a little.

KATRINA: Let me see.

PETE: Come on, Zeke. Let's go.

MUTTON: *(Picking up the pumpkin:)* See you at the party, Brom.

(Sleepy Hollow Boys exit.)

KATRINA: Brom, tonight is the engagement party for Ichabod and me.

(Brom whacks his anvil.)

Aunt Helga would like to use the new kettle, if you can have it ready by then.

(Brom whacks the anvil again.)

Could you bring it to the house before the party? Brom?

BROM: If you want.

KATRINA: I hope you'll stay and join us for the celebration. The whole town will be there.

BROM: I'll try.

(Ichabod enters.)

ICHABOD: Katrina, my dearest. How are the preparations for our engagement party?

KATRINA: Aunt Helga is so excited. She's been cooking and cleaning all week!

ICHABOD: Dear Aunt Helga. And lovely little Wanda. We certainly shall miss them when they return to Pennsylvania.

KATRINA: Yes, we will.

ICHABOD: Well, then. If you are ready to return home, I would be happy to escort you through the forest.

KATRINA: That's so thoughtful. But Aunt Helga isn't ready for visitors yet. I'll see you this evening!

(Katrina exits.)

ICHABOD: Yes. This evening...

(Brom goes back to work.)

Well, then.

(Brom whacks his anvil.)

Mr. Bones. You fashion a cornucopia of paraphernalia from the ferrous metal, do you not?

BROM: What?

ICHABOD: *(Casually:)* Iron amulets, for example. Perhaps you make iron amulets.

BROM: Now, Professor Crane.   Why would you want to know about iron amulets?

ICHABOD: Or horseshoes, perhaps? You do sell horseshoes.

BROM: Professor Crane, you don't have a horse.

ICHABOD: Iron nails, then. Or bells!

BROM: 'Fraid I'm fresh out of bells. All this talk about the Headless Horseman. You know how superstitious us locals are.

ICHABOD: Do you have anything made out of iron? Anything at all?

BROM: Only this kettle. And I'm bringing it to Miss Van Tassel's house tonight.

ICHABOD: Mr. Bones. I, too, must travel to the Van Tassel estate. And I have not enjoyed the pleasure of your company since my arrival in this pastoral haven. Would you join me in a carefree jaunt through the forest?

BROM: Gee, Professor. Tonight is All Hallow's Eve.

ICHABOD: I know.

BROM: I'm not an educated man like you are. I'd be afraid to walk through the forest on All Hallow's Eve. I'm going to ride my horse!

(Brom exits.)

ICHABOD: Mr. Bones. Mr. Bones!

(Ichabod stands alone in the square. Suddenly the bright light of the town square dims, and ominous shadows fall across the stage. Ichabod is plunged into the depths of the forest.)

(MUSIC up. Segue to Scene 2.)

SCENE 2

(The Forest. The Forest Voices sound more shrill, more ominous than before. Leaves and underbrush tremble in the wind. Ichabod cautiously makes his way down the path.)

The Forest Song - Part 2

VOICE: *(Like a raccoon:)* CH-CH-CH-CH-CH-CH. CH-CH-CH-CH-CH-CH.

VOICE: *(Like an owl:)* WHO, WHO.

ICHABOD: That's right. I am an educated man.

VOICE: *(Baying like a wolf:)* AROO!

ICHABOD: Educated men do not believe in demons.

VOICES: DEMONS...

ICHABOD: Educated men do not believe in ghosts.

VOICES: DARKNESS...

ICHABOD: Educated men do not believe in darkness!

(A deep male VOICE laughs eerily.)

VOICE: HA-HA-HA-HA!

ICHABOD: No, what I meant to say is that educated —

VOICES: *(Cutting off Ichabod:)* IS THERE SOMETHING TO FEAR IN THE FOREST?

I'm Not Afraid - Part 2

ICHABOD: OH, I'M NOT AFRAID OF THE HORSEMAN,
A DEAD MAN WILL ALWAYS STAY DEAD.
SO THERE'S NOT A REASON TO PANIC;
THERE'S NO SENSE LOSING MY HEAD.
SO WHERE SHOULD I BE AFRAID?

NOWHERE.
OF WHOM SHOULD I BE AFRAID?
NO ONE.
AND WHEN SHOULD I BE AFRAID?
NEVER.
NOWHERE. NO ONE. NEVER. NOT I!

(We hear the SOUND of BUSHES RUSTLING and see something move in the underbrush. The "HORSEMAN MOTIVE" plays.)

What's that? Who's there?

(A BAT swoops across Ichabod's path.)

VOICE: *(Like a bat:)* EEK! EEK!

(The bat circles and swoops toward Ichabod again.)

ICHABOD: Get away from me! Get away! Get away!

(Ichabod thrashes about wildly, then flees in terror. As he exits we may see the glimpse of a shadow or a silhouette moving through the bushes.)

SCENE CHANGE MUSIC: Act 2 Scene Change 2 to 3

(After a brief pause, the Sleepy Hollow Boys appear grinning and begin to change the set. Segue to Scene 3.)

SCENE 3

(The Van Tassel Home. Helga whirls about nervously. She carries a large plate of turnovers. Wanda follows her instructions.)

HELGA: Wanda, put the flowers on the table. No, on the other table!

WANDA: Mother...

HELGA: Is that a spot on the tablecloth?

WANDA: Watch out for the flowers!

HELGA: Decorations! I need more decorations!

WANDA: Careful, Mother, or you'll drop the—

HELGA: *(Dropping the platter:)* Oh, no! The turnovers!

WANDA: I'll go get the broom.

(Wanda exits. MUSIC up.)

HELGA: Oh, dear. The guests will be here any minute. Why do I feel like there's something I forgot to do? I washed the windows. I planned the party games. *(Picking up a turnover:)* I hope there's nothing I forgot to cook!

Helga's Menu

HELGA: I MADE APPLESAUCE WITH CINNAMON
AND APPLESAUCE WITH CLOVE,
AND THREE OTHER KINDS OF APPLESAUCE
ARE COOKING ON THE STOVE.
I MADE CANDY APPLE DUMPLINGS
TOPPED WITH APPLE HONEY FLUFF;
I ROLLED EACH ONE IN SUGAR,
SO I HOPE THEY'RE SWEET ENOUGH.
I MADE CRISPY APPLE FRITTERS;

LIKE THE KIND THEY SERVE DOWN SOUTH.
AND I ROASTED AN ENTIRE PIG
WITH AN APPLE IN ITS MOUTH.
I MADE APPLE OYSTER CRUMBLE
TOPPED WITH APPLE-ONION SWIRLS.
I MADE LIMA BEANS WITH CIDER SAUCE
AND LITTLE APPLE CURLS.
I'VE BEEN COOKING WITH ALL MY MIGHT
DISHES FOR EVERY APPETITE.
IS THERE SOMETHING I SHOULD HAVE COOKED?
SOMETHING I'VE OVERLOOKED?
I MADE APPLE-GARLIC DOUGHNUTS
AND AN APPLE-HERRING LOG.
I MADE APPLEKRAUT WITH CODFISH,
AND A BOWL OF APPLE NOG.
I HOPE EV'RYONE LIKES APPLES,
BUT SUPPOSE SOME PEOPLE DON'T!
ALL THOSE FOLKS WHO DON'T LIKE APPLES
SITTING SILENT IN THEIR CHAIRS;
BLAMING ME FOR EMPTY STOMACHS;
GIVING ME RESENTFUL STARES.
WAIT A MINUTE, THERE'S NO PROBLEM.
'CAUSE I ALSO MADE FIVE KINDS OF...PEARS!

(Speaks:)

Oh, dear. Maybe there's still time to roast a chicken!

(MUSIC ends as Katrina enters.)

KATRINA: Aunt Helga, do I look all right?

HELGA: Katrina, I am so, so sorry.

KATRINA: What's wrong?

HELGA: I've ruined your engagement party. It's going to be a disaster!

KATRINA: I'm sure it will be wonderful.

HELGA: No, it won't. I ruined the menu, I didn't plan enough party games, and I never did wash the walls!

KATRINA: None of that matters.

HELGA: Yes, it does. I'm no help to you at all. It's a good thing I'm going home next week. You'll be much better off when I'm gone.

KATRINA: Aunt Helga...

HELGA: You'll be glad to be rid of me, won't you.

KATRINA: How can you say that? I never would have made it through the last few months without you! As a matter of fact...I've been wondering... Instead of going back home to your farm, would you consider staying here in Sleepy Hollow?

HELGA: You want me to stay?

KATRINA: I know it's asking a lot. But there's plenty of room in the house, if you don't mind. And it would mean so much to me if you could be here for the wedding.

HELGA: You mean, I could stay in this beautiful house? Wanda could keep going to school?

KATRINA: I will miss you so much if you go.

HELGA: Thank you, Katrina! I promise I'll make this up to you. I'll plan a big party for your wedding. With a cake five layers high. And I'll sew the dress myself!

(Ichabod stumbles in, breathing heavily. He is still clutching the stick.)

ICHABOD: Am I still in one piece?

HELGA: *(To Ichabod:)* Professor Crane, what do you like best? Chocolate frosting, or butter cream?

WANDA: Mother, I smell something burning.

HELGA: Oh, no! The crabapple casserole!

(Helga tears offstage.)

ICHABOD: Get me a glass of water.

KATRINA: *(Pouring the water:)* Ichabod, what happened?

ICHABOD: I was attacked! In the forest!

WANDA: It was the Headless Horseman. You saw the Headless Horseman!

ICHABOD: Water, quickly!

KATRINA: *(Giving Ichabod a glass:)* Here.

WANDA: Did you see his face? It's creepy, isn't it—the way he carries his head under his arm?

ICHABOD: Be quiet!

WANDA: He rides fast, doesn't he? And the horse sounds so gruesome when he's closing in on you.

ICHABOD: Be quiet!

WANDA: Did he reach out with his cold, clammy hands? Did he grab you by your shirt and try to pull you—

ICHABOD: *(Not letting her finish:)* I said silence, you little brat!

(Ichabod slaps Wanda across the face or shakes her violently.)

WANDA: *(Gasping in fear:)* Oh!

KATRINA: Ichabod!

ICHABOD: There is no such thing as the Headless Horseman! Do you hear me? I was attacked by a bat—not some outlandish fantasy!

WANDA: *(Running to Katrina:)* Katrina...

ICHABOD: How dare you invent such monstrous lies! I'll make sure no one in this town ever listens to you again!

KATRINA: Ichabod, that's enough!

(Wanda bursts into tears and exits.)

ICHABOD: I want her out of the house tomorrow! Her and that useless mother of hers.

KATRINA: I thought you loved Aunt Helga!

ICHABOD: As soon as we're married, I'm moving as far away from this miserable little town as I can get.

KATRINA: Miserable?

ICHABOD: I'll sell the farm, and the livestock...

KATRINA: But who will teach the children?

ICHABOD: The children can die in ignorance for all I care! This house ought to fetch a pretty penny.

KATRINA: Wait...

ICHABOD: I'll buy a house in Boston. With lots of servants. And my own private library...

KATRINA: We are not selling my father's house!

ICHABOD: My dear, you are in no position to decide. Once we are married, I will hold legal title to everything you own. And I will dispose of it as I please.

KATRINA: If you don't want to stay in Sleepy Hollow...then I'm calling off our engagement!

ICHABOD: As you wish. I shall simply sue you for breach of promise. It will all be mine, whether you marry me or not.

SOFIE (O.S.): Yoo-hoo! Professor Crane!

ICHABOD: *(Extending his hand to Katrina:)* Well, Miss Van Tassel. Shall we greet our guests?

(Katrina exits wordlessly as the Townspeople enter.)

TOWNSPEOPLE: Professor Crane! Congratulations! When's the happy day?

(Lights down on the Van Tassel home. Lights up on the garden outside.)

<u>SCENE CHANGE MUSIC: With Him (Act II Scene 3 to 4)</u>

SCENE 4

(The Van Tassel Garden. Katrina runs into the garden. The SCENE CHANGE MUSIC continues as underscoring.)

KATRINA: This can't be happening. He seemed so perfect! *(The enormity of it all sinking in:)* What have I done?

(As the UNDERSCORING finishes, Brom enters.)

BROM: Here's your kettle.

KATRINA: Just put it over there.

(Katrina paces and fidgets with the lace on her sleeves as in Act I, Scene 1.)

BROM: Something's wrong, isn't it.

KATRINA: Whatever makes you say that?

BROM: You always — fidget — when you're upset.

KATRINA: Oh, Brom! I am so stupid!

BROM: Stupid?

KATRINA: Stupid and blind...

BROM: You're the smartest person I know!

KATRINA: I've ruined everything! The school, the library, the church choir...

BROM: *(Fumbling in his pocket:)* Here, take my handkerchief.

(Katrina takes the handkerchief from Brom.)

KATRINA: Everything Father worked for. Everything he wanted to give to this town. I've lost it all.

BROM: You'll make it better.

(MUSIC up as Brom speaks.)

KATRINA: No, Brom. I won't.

BROM: You'll think of a way to fix things.

KATRINA: It's too late, Brom. I can't.

BROM: Of course you can. You can do anything you set your mind to.

KATRINA: You don't know what I've done!

BROM: But Katrina, I know *you*.

I Know You By Heart

BROM: I KNOW YOU BY HEART.
I KNOW ALL YOUR WAYS.
I KNOW THAT YOU LIKE TO SEE YOUR BREATH ON
CHILLY DAYS.
I KNOW YOU LOVE WILLOW TREES.
I KNOW YOU HATE BUTTERSCOTCH.
WHEN YOU'RE NERVOUS, YOU TUG AT THE LACE ON
YOUR SLEEVES.
I KNOW YOU BY HEART.
I SEE YOU ALL YEAR.
I SEE HOW YOU LOOK AT STARS WHEN WINTER
NIGHTS ARE CLEAR.
IN SPRING, YOU CHASE BUTTERFLIES.
IN SUMMER, YOU BRAID YOUR HAIR.
IN AUTUMN, YOU LIKE TO WALK ON CRUNCHY
FALLEN LEAVES.
BUT I DON'T KNOW
WHY YOU DON'T KNOW HOW STRONG YOU ARE.
ANY PERSON YOU EVER MET WOULD SURELY TELL YOU
SO.
AND I DON'T SEE
HOW YOU EVER COULD DOUBT YOURSELF.

NOT WHEN YOU ARE MORE WONDERFUL THAN
ANYONE I KNOW.
I KNOW YOU BY HEART
YOU'RE PART OF EACH DAY.
YOU'RE PART OF EACH STEP I TAKE AND EV'RY WORD I
SAY.
YOU'RE THERE WHEN I CLOSE MY EYES.
I COULD SKETCH YOU FROM MEMORY.
YOUR FACE IS THE FACE I WANT TO GAZE AT ALL MY
LIFE.
YOU'RE THERE IN MY SOUL.
YOU'RE HERE ON MY MIND.
I KNOW YOU BY HEART.

KATRINA: *(Basking in the warmth of Brom's words:)* Is that
really how you see me? *(Singing:)* I NEVER KNEW...

I Know You By Heart (Continued – Duet)

...THAT A MAN COULD SURPRISE ME SO;
THAT A MAN WHO'S SO SHY COULD BE SO PASSIONATE
INSIDE.
I ALWAYS THOUGHT
I WAS ONLY A FRIEND TO YOU.
WON'T YOU HELP ME TO UNDERSTAND THE POET'S
HEART YOU HIDE?
TO KNOW YOU BY HEART...

BROM: TO SPEND TIME WITH YOU...

KATRINA: TO NOW GET ACQUAINTED WITH THE MAN
I THOUGHT I KNEW.

BROM: TO SEE US AS MORE THAN FRIENDS?
TO SEE HOW OUR STORY ENDS.

BROM & KATRINA: I THINK THAT RIGHT HERE AND NOW IS THE PERFECT PLACE TO START...

KATRINA: TO KNOW YOU

BROM: LIKE I KNOW YOU

BROM & KATRINA: TO KNOW YOU BY HEART.

(Brom and Katrina kiss. Suddenly there is a bloodcurdling SCREAM from offstage.))

WANDA (O.S.): *(Screaming as if in pain:)* Aaaaahhhhhhh!

BROM: What was that?

(Wanda enters, hobbling. She carries a small bundle of clothes.)

WANDA: I tripped! I think I broke my toe!

KATRINA: Wanda, why aren't you at the party?

WANDA: The way Professor Crane just hit me? I'm getting as far away from that maniac as I can!

BROM: He hit her?

KATRINA: He's not the man he pretends to be.

WANDA: Yeah. That creep is only marrying Katrina for her money.

BROM: He's what?

KATRINA: And if I don't marry him, it's breach of promise and he'll take everything I own.

BROM: I oughtta clobber that little rat.

KATRINA: No, Brom. Promise me you won't.

WANDA: I know! Let's all run away together! Katrina, you could teach school. Brom, I could help you with the blacksmithing! I know a lot about iron!

BROM: Katrina loves Sleepy Hollow. She can't let Professor Crane run her out of town.

KATRINA: You're right, Brom. I can't just run away.

(The Sleepy Hollow Boys enter.)

ZEKE: Hey, Brom! What are you doing out here? The party's inside!

(Helga enters.)

HELGA: Come in, Katrina. Everyone wants to congratulate you.

(Lights up on the Van Tassel home as Katrina, Brom and Wanda are dragged inside.)

SCENE 5

(The Van Tassel Home. The Townspeople crowd around Ichabod.)

ANNA: Congratulations, Professor Crane!   This is such a happy occasion!

ICHABOD: *(Kissing Anna's hand:)* Made happier yet by your presence.   As the poet said, "Good company and good discourse are the very sinews of virtue."

(Katrina, Brom, Wanda, Helga and Zeke enter.)

HELGA: Here's the bride-to-be!

SOFIE: Congratulations, Miss Van Tassel!   We are so excited about the wedding!

ANNA: I'm going to make you a pair of new shoes for your wedding day.

SOFIE: And I've spoken with everyone in the church choir. We're going to learn a new hymn to sing at the service.

KATRINA: Thank you, Sofie. But—

CHRIS: Next spring, after the wedding, Brom and I can help you build the town a library.

KATRINA: Thank you, Chris—

CHRIS: *(Cutting off Katrina:)* A toast!   To Katrina Van Tassel, the most generous woman in Sleepy Hollow.

TOWNSPEOPLE: Here, here!   Congratulations!   To Miss Van Tassel!   Many years of happiness!

KATRINA: No!   Stop!   Thank you for your kindness and good wishes.   But there's something I need to tell you.   About the wedding...   About the church choir, and the library...

(Suddenly there is a FLASH of lightning, followed by the SOUND of a HORSE WHINNYING AND REARING.)

ICHABOD: What was that?

ANNA: It's the Headless Horseman!

HELGA: Bar the doors! Lock the windows!

WANDA: No! Get your horseshoes and your bells. If you don't have anything made of iron, grab some salt! A pinch of salt keeps the spirits away!

(Guests start to follow Wanda's orders.)

ICHABOD: Stop it, all of you! You there, Chris. Look out the window. Do you see anything outside?

CHRIS: There's a full moon.

ICHABOD: Do you see a ghost?

CHRIS: I don't see him...

ICHABOD: Well, then. That noise must have been one of the horses in the barn. There is no such thing as a Headless Horseman!

ANNA: But Wanda saw him!

SOFIE & OTHERS: That's right! Just last week! Wanda saw him!

ICHABOD: She lied, you half-witted bumpkins! If you believe her, you're as ignorant as she is!

ANNA: I beg your pardon!

ICHABOD: Terrifying people with her outrageous fabrications. Don't listen to a word she says!

WANDA: Someday you'll believe me, Professor Crane. Someday he's going to come for you!

KATRINA: *(Getting an idea:)* That's right. Wanda is right. You've got to be careful, Ichabod. We don't want to lose another schoolmaster.

ICHABOD: What do you mean, lose a schoolmaster?

KATRINA: The way we lost the last one. We all know what happened to poor Nicholas Vedder.

TOWNSPEOPLE: *(All at once:)* That's right! How horrible! The old schoolmaster. You know the story.

BROM: That's right. He was an educated man, just like you, Professor Crane.

KATRINA: It was All Hallow's Eve, just like tonight. Nicholas Vedder was walking through the forest, when he heard the most terrifying sound you can imagine...

The Legend

IT WAS COLD THAT NIGHT
AND THE MILKY LIGHT
OF THE MOON WAS EERIE AND BLEAK.
AS THE TEACHER STRODE
ON THE COUNTRY ROAD,
HE COULD HEAR A HORRIBLE SHRIEK.
BUT HE SHRUGGED AND GRINNED;

BROM: IT WAS JUST THE WIND,

KATRINA & BROM: SO HE PULLED AT THE RUMPLED HAT HE ALWAYS WORE.

ICHABOD: It was only the wind, wasn't it?

(Katrina and Brom exchange glances.)

KATRINA: THEN HE FELT THE FORCE
OF A MIGHTY HORSE

AND HE TURNED AND SHIVERED WITH DREAD.

BROM: HE COULD SEE NO TRACE
OF THE HORSEMAN'S FACE
FOR THE MAN WAS MINUS A HEAD.

KATRINA & BROM: AND THE TEACHER KNEW
IT WAS OLD VAN *(Rhymes with "knew":)* BRUGH
WHO HAD COME BACK TO LIFE TO SETTLE UP THE
SCORE.

ENSEMBLE (MINUS ICHABOD): INTO THE NIGHT, THE
TEACHER AND THE HORSEMAN RACED;
OVER THE GLEN, THEY WENT LIKE FOX AND HOUND.
WAY UP THE ROAD, THE TEACHER SAW THE OLD
CHURCH BRIDGE;
REACH THE BRIDGE AND HE'D BE SAFE AND SOUND.

ICHABOD: Then what happened?

KATRINA: AS THE TEACHER RAN,
HE COULD FEEL A HAND
AS IT GRABBED THE TAILS OF HIS COAT.

ENSEMBLE (MINUS ICHABOD): HIS COAT!

BROM: WHEN HE NEARED THE RIDGE
RIGHT BEFORE THE BRIDGE,
HE COULD FEEL THE HAND AT HIS THROAT.

ENSEMBLE (MINUS ICHABOD): HIS THROAT!

BROM: AND HE TRIED TO SHOUT

KATRINA: BUT NO SOUND CAME OUT;
AND THE HORSEMAN BURST INTO FLAMES AS BRIGHT
AS DAWN.

ENSEMBLE (MINUS ICHABOD): OH, THE TOWN WAS
VEXED

ON THE MONDAY NEXT
FOR THE TEACHER PLUMB DISAPPEARED
WHEN THEY LED THE SEARCH
TO THE OLD GRAY CHURCH,
WHAT THEY FOUND WAS GRUESOME AND WEIRD:

KATRINA: HE WAS LAID OUT FLAT

BROM: AND HE WORE HIS HAT

KATRINA & BROM: ON HIS SHOULDERS BECAUSE

ENSEMBLE (TENORS, SOPRANOS): ON HIS SHOULDERS BECAUSE

ENSEMBLE (ALTOS, BASSES): ON HIS SHOULDERS BECAUSE

ENSEMBLE (MINUS ICHABOD): THE TEACHER'S HEAD WAS GONE!

ICHABOD: *(Screaming:)* NO!

HELGA: Well! Does anyone want to bob for apples?

(Once again, there is the SOUND of a HORSE WHINNYING.)

BROM: Come on, boys. We'd better get my horse, and ride back to town. It's nearly midnight.

ICHABOD: Midnight?!

CHRIS & ANNA: Run for your lives!

ICHABOD: Wait! What about me? Give me that salt!

(Ichabod dives on the salt shaker. The Guests scatter, taking the Van Tassel Home set pieces with them as they exit. Ichabod is left alone on stage. Lights dim, shadows loom, and we segue to the Forest. MUSIC up. Segue to Scene 6.)

SCENE 6

(The Forest. Ichabod stands alone as the forest is created around him. This time we may see that the VOICES he hears come from the actors who play the Townspeople and the Sleepy Hollow Boys. This time the actors playing Katrina, Brom, Helga and Wanda might also join the Voice in song:)

The Forest Song - Part 3

VOICE: *(Like a raccoon, chattering directly into Ichabod's ear, then hiding:)* CH-CH-CH-CH-CH-CH.

VOICE: *(Like a wolf, popping out from behind a tree, then hiding:)* AROO!

VOICE: *(Like a crow, popping up from behind a bush, then hiding:)* CAW, CAW.

ICHABOD: There is no such thing as the Headless Horseman!

VOICE: *(Moaning like the wind:)* OHHHHHH!

ICHABOD: It's only the wind.

VOICES: IT'S NOT THE WIND.

ICHABOD: This isn't really happening.

VOICES: OH, YES IT IS.

ICHABOD: It's just my mind playing tricks on me.

VOICES: OH, NO IT'S NOT.

ICHABOD: There is nothing out there!

VOICES: DID SOMETHING MOVE?

ICHABOD: What moved? Leave me alone!

VOICES: IS THERE SOMETHING TO FEAR IN THE FOREST?

I'm Not Afraid - Part 3

ICHABOD: OH, I'M NOT AFRAID OF THE DEMON
THAT DWELLS IN THE DARK, SO THEY SAY;
FOR I HAVE SOME SALT IN MY POCKET
TO DRIVE THAT DEMON AWAY.
SO WHERE SHOULD I BE AFRAID?

(During the above, a figure on horseback enters. It is, of course, the HEADLESS HORSEMAN. The Horseman is terrifying to behold, although on closer examination he may look like a man being carried by two other people, with a large cape over his head and a jack-o'-lantern under one arm.)

VOICES, GROUP 1: NOWHERE.

ICHABOD: OF WHOM SHOULD I BE AFRAID?

VOICES, GROUP 2: NO ONE.

ICHABOD: AND...WHEN SHOULD I BE AFRAID?

HEADLESS HORSEMAN: NOW!

The Forest Chase

(Ichabod shrieks in terror as the Horseman chases him off. The Forest Voices go wild.)

ICHABOD: Help me! Save me!

(As Ichabod tries to escape, the Horseman and the VOICES in the forest taunt him, block his path, pop out from behind trees to scare him, etc. The entire Ensemble participates in the chase: entering and exiting through the aisles of the theater, running under and behind the audience's seats, and generally breaking the fourth wall as much as possible. The chase might begin in slow motion, then get faster and faster as the music builds.)

HEADLESS HORSEMAN & VOICES: NO TIME TO THINK!
DANGER, THROAT, CORPSE

JUST TURN AND RUN!
VENGEANCE, DOOM, DEATH
THERE'S A GHOUL ON THE WAY.
YOU'RE A FOOL IF YOU STAY.
DON'T TURN AROUND!
TORTURE, TRAP, BLOOD
HE'S AT YOUR HEELS!
SAVE—YOUR—NECK.
DOES THE THUMP OF YOUR HEART
MAKE YOU JUMP WITH A START?
YOU BETTER FLEE!
THIS—WAY—OUT
AND DON'T COME BACK.
RUN—RUN—RUN
FEEL A JOLT OF PURE FRIGHT
AS YOU BOLT THROUGH THE NIGHT
WITH A SHATTERING YELL
LIKE A BAT OUT OF HELL.
AS YOU'RE GETTING AWAY
DON'T FORGET HOW TO PRAY.
SO BEWARE OF THE DEAD
AND TAKE CARE OF YOUR HEAD!

ICHABOD: *(Screaming:)* Run awaaayyyyyy!!!

> *(Ichabod tears offstage, dropping his hat on the ground. The Headless Horseman hurls his "head" at the departing schoolmaster. Blackout.)*

SCENE 7

(The Forest. Lights slowly rise. The forest is empty now, except for Brom, who sits in the clearing reading a book, and Ichabod's hat, which still lies where it fell. The Sleepy Hollow Boys enter.)

PETE: *(To the audience:)* So Katrina got to keep her father's house.

(As Pete speaks, Katrina enters. She goes to Brom, takes his hand, and pulls him to his feet.)

MUTTON: Brom got to keep Katrina.

(Katrina and Brom embrace, then exit.)

ZEKE: Aunt Helga got to bake a wedding cake.

(Helga and Wanda cross carrying an enormous wedding cake.)

PETE: And Sleepy Hollow got the library, the hymnals, and a new teacher the following year.

(MUSIC up.)

ZEKE: As for Ichabod Crane...

Welcome to Sleepy Hollow (Second Act Finale Reprise)

SLEEPY HOLLOW BOYS: WE CAN GUESS AT WHAT YOU'RE BOUND TO SAY
IT'S A COMMON QUESTION HERE IN SLEEPY HOLLOW:

(Pete strolls forward and picks up Ichabod's hat.)

"IS IT TRUE THAT ICHABOD WAS ROBBED OF HIS HEAD?"

PETE: *(Waving the hat:)* HE NEVER SAID.

SLEEPY HOLLOW BOYS: SO BE CAREFUL HEADING HOME TODAY.

YOU MAY MEET THE HORSEMAN ON THE PATH YOU
FOLLOW.

IF YOU DO, JUST TELL HIM HE'S A PAIN IN THE NECK...

(Zeke puts his hands around his neck:)

AND RUN LIKE HECK!

*(SOUND of a DEEP, OMINOUS LAUGH offstage. It starts
softly at first, then grows louder and louder.)*

PETE: Cut that out.

ZEKE: What?

PETE: That laugh.

ZEKE: I'm not laughing!

*(The Boys pause and listen. A severed head rolls on from
offstage ... or maybe it's a pumpkin. MANIACAL LAUGHTER
fills the theater.)*

SLEEPY HOLLOW BOYS: Run awayyyyy!!!!!!

*(Lightning flashes. The Sleepy Hollow Boys run offstage.
Something drops from the ceiling into the audience's field of
vision: bats, cobwebs, skeletons... Perhaps a headless figure
appears in the background. The LAUGHTER CRESCENDOS.)*

(Blackout. End of Act II.)

BOWS

(If desired, the INSTRUMENTAL MUSIC to "Great Day in the Morning" can play as the Cast takes their bows. If desired, after bows are done the Cast may sing the following:)

OPTIONAL BOWS MUSIC: Great Day in the Morning (Second Act Finale Reprise)

ENSEMBLE: EACH NIGHT IN THE AUTUMN,
A HEADLESS MAN ON HORSE APPEARS.
SOME PEOPLE HAVE THOUGHT 'IM
TO MERELY BE PRETEND.
BUT HE RIDES EACH AUTUMN,
STILL TAKING HEADS AS SOUVENIRS.
BEWARE IN THE AUTUMN;
HE'S VERY REAL, MY FRIEND!

(Finis.)

The Authors Speak

What inspired you to write this play?

OWEN KALT: I wanted to write a musical based on Washington Irving's *The Legend of Sleepy Hollow* because I have always loved old-fashioned ghost stories and because my favorite holiday as a child was Halloween. I had seen many enjoyable adaptations of Irving's short story, but I had never seen a good full-length musical based on it. I knew from the start that we would face certain problems in adapting this work. Specifically, the original short story is only about 45 pages long, so I knew we would have to expand on that material. Moreover, I knew that people in the audience would have certain expectations, which our show would have to meet. Audience members would expect to see a spooky forest, a headless rider and a romantic triangle in which a young woman must choose between a brainy man and a brawny man. Translating those elements to the stage turned out to be more difficult than I originally imagined. Upon reading and re-reading the short story, I gradually realized that Washington Irving did not create any sympathetic characters for his yarn. All the main characters are selfish, manipulative, and/or domineering. Don't get me wrong, I am not criticizing Mr. Irving's story, which I consider to be brilliant. But the same elements that work beautifully in a short story don't necessarily make for a satisfying musical play. After giving this a lot of thought, I decided that we should give our audience a reason to "root for" one or more of the characters. Schoolmaster Ichabod Crane is the most famous character in the story, so my initial thought was that Ichabod should be our show's protagonist. In order to make that work, I felt that we would have to make him more sympathetic. But so much of what makes Ichabod enjoyable is that he is not only a pretentious coward, he is also a schoolteacher who hates children. He is a character we love to hate. After more thought, I surprised my collaborators by suggesting that we make Ichabod the show's antagonist. The position of "protagonist" would be shared by two characters: Katrina Van Tassel and Brom Bones. I wanted our play to be a musical comedy, as well as a spook show, so I proposed to my collaborators that we make Katrina and Brom into "nicer" versions of themselves. That way, the audience would root for Katrina and Brom to find love with each other. That would also give the audience an extra reason to enjoy watching The Headless Horseman scare Ichabod Crane out of town— because Katrina should wind up in Brom's embrace instead of Ichabod's. It is with great pride that I report that audiences who have seen our musical version of *Sleepy Hollow* have confirmed that my choices were correct.

ELIZABETH DOYLE: I did handsprings at the prospect of bringing this beloved American classic to the musical stage when Owen approached me. I knew we worked well together as he had done some lyric fixes for a previous show of mine, and we had written a bang-up opening for a revue presented during the 1996 Chicago Democratic Presidential election with the line "We had so much fun the last time, let's do it all again." Taking the classic tale and adding flesh and humor to the characters was our initial quest. In the indispensable sessions we did at the ASCAP/Disney Musical Theater Workshop in California, Stephen Schwartz counseled me to keep my musical voice but add color from the time period in which we were setting our piece, sage advice which helped me take the score to a higher level. Theatre Building Chicago's writing workshop provided us with a ready talent pool of playwrights from which to choose, Scott Sandoe being our initial scribe, handing off to our ultimate bookwriter Judy Freed.

JUDY FREED: Owen, Elizabeth and I met in the musical theater writers' workshop at Theatre Building Chicago. *Sleepy Hollow* began with another bookwriter—Scott Sandoe—who left the project when he moved to Los Angeles. After Scott left, Elizabeth and Owen wrote "I Know You By Heart"—a gorgeous song that had a very different tone from Scott's script and didn't really fit the structure. When Owen and Elizabeth asked me to join the project, "I Know You By Heart" became my inspiration. I decided to write a new book that built up to "I Know You By Heart," which would be a major turning point in Act II. This decision sparked a series of new directions: Brom would be unable to tell Katrina how he felt about her because of the disparity in their incomes and educations; Katrina would be unaware of Brom's feelings because of her preoccupation with her father's death and her fear that she couldn't live up to his legacy; and Ichabod would take advantage of the whole situation by manipulating Katrina with beautiful words before eventually displaying his true colors.

Sleepy Hollow was developed at Theatre Building Chicago and at the ASCAP/Disney Musical Theater Workshop, where it received guidance from composer/lyricist Stephen Schwartz. During the development process, the show continued to evolve with the addition of new songs and the creation of a new subplot involving Wanda, Katrina's ghoul-loving younger cousin.

Have you dealt with the same theme in other works that you have written?
We've all adapted other literary works into musicals. Elizabeth and Owen's adaptation of *The Virginian* (book by Donald Abramson) was commissioned by Theatre Building Chicago and was presented at the Stages 2000 festival of new

musicals. *Emma & Company*, Judy's adaptation of Edna Ferber's Emma McChesney stories (music and lyrics by Jon Steinhagen) was produced in New York and was named a *BackStage* "theatrical highlight of 2001."

What writers have had the most profound effect on your style?
OWEN KALT: My lyric writing style is influenced by my admiration for the cleverness of Cole Porter and Lorenz Hart.

ELIZABETH DOYLE: The whole Great American Songbook has provided my musical theatre education. Lyricists such as Dorothy Fields, Yip Harburg, Johnny Mercer as well as composers such as Richard Rodgers, Charles Strouse, Harold Arlen and George Gershwin, among many others, continue to delight and inform me.

JUDY FREED: It's hard to choose just a few. There are so many wonderful playwrights and musical theatre bookwriters!

What inspired you to become a playwright?
OWEN KALT: I was inspired to become a lyricist by my discovery that people found my jokes much funnier when the jokes rhymed and were set to music.

ELIZABETH DOYLE: My mother was mad for musicals, operettas and opera. Being exposed to such theatrical music at an early age, I started presenting stories with music in our basement and garage for neighbor kids. My local community theatre in Sioux Falls, South Dakota had a fantastic theatre program so I sang, acted, danced, learned how to build sets, how to apply make-up and music directed before entering secondary school. Senior year, my alma mater, O'Gorman High School put on its first musical under the direction of a theatre whiz named Nancy Wheeler. I won the role of Sarah Brown in *Guys and Dolls* and was permanently made a member of the "mad for musicals club." I have been involved in either music directing or writing musicals ever since.

JUDY FREED: I love collaborating with talented people. Writing book for musicals lets me collaborate with so many talented artists.

How was the first production different from the vision that you created in your mind?
OWEN KALT: An early developmental production was notable for the absence of a Headless Horseman!

ELIZABETH DOYLE: I had only heard the score with solo piano up until the first two simultaneous productions. Theatre-Hikes had an electric piano rigged up on a child's wagon festooned with fake leaves so the music director could move the music from scene to scene in the great outdoors. Somehow, the director had found talented actors who also played portable instruments such as guitar, violin and flute. Acorn Theater had actually orchestrated my piano score to accommodate a small combo and fantastic theater organ. Both productions let me hear things I had never heard in the score before.

JUDY FREED: We had two simultaneous "first productions." One, by Chicago-based Theatre-Hikes, was staged at outdoor venues across the Chicago area. The other, by Michigan's Acorn Theater, was a sophisticated puppet show combining elements of shadow and bunraku puppetry. I had always envisioned the show as a traditional theatre piece. It was thrilling to see two non-traditional productions of our show in the same season—and to see that two very different interpretations and presentations both worked!

About the Authors

Judy Freed has seen her plays and musicals performed in London, New York, Chicago, California, Washington, Massachusetts, and throughout the Midwest. Her writing has been recognized by such organizations as the National Music Theater Conference and the American Alliance for Theatre & Education. Musicals include *Sleepy Hollow* (developed at the ASCAP/Disney Musical Theater Workshop), *Emma & Company* (named a Back Stage "Theatrical Highlight of 2001"), *Through the Door* (presented at Trafalgar Studios, London), *Mom! The Musical* (selected for the TRU Voices New Musicals Series), and *Somebody Else's Troubles* (featuring the songs of Grammy-winner Steve Goodman). Four of her plays for young readers have been published by Pearson Scott Foresman. She is a member of The Dramatists Guild and the International Center for Women Playwrights.

Elizabeth Doyle wears several hats: composer, lyricist, singer, pianist, arranger and music director. Her single songs have been featured in New York ASCAP new music programs, Minneapolis' Cafe Latte Da, in the Chicago Humanities Festival, *Death: The Musical* in Houston (TX) and at various Chicago venues such as Park West, Maxim's, Victory Gardens and Preston Bradley in the Culturual Center. Her chamber music was performed at the Paradiso in Amsterdam. Some of her other musicals include *Fat Tuesday*, *Alice In Analysis*, *The Virginian*, *The White City* and *Duo*, performed at the famed Steppenwolf Theatre. A featured singer/pianist on Marian McPartland's NPR program Piano Jazz, Doyle was a magnet for many years at Chicago's famed Pump Room and has performed throughout the United States and Europe. She has two CDs available, *Elizabeth Doyle* and *Time Flies*. Her website is: www.elizabethdoylemusic.com.

Owen Kalt is a Chicago-based lyricist. In addition to *Sleepy Hollow*, he wrote the lyrics for *Belle Barth: If I Embarrass You, Tell Your Friends*, which has been produced in Chicago. He also wrote the lyrics for *American Klezmer*, which has been produced in Los Angeles.

About YouthPLAYS

YouthPLAYS (www.youthplays.com) is a publisher of award-winning professional dramatists and talented new discoveries, each with an original theatrical voice, and all dedicated to expanding the vocabulary of theatre for young actors and audiences. On our website you'll find one-act and full-length plays and musicals for teen and pre-teen (and even college) actors, as well as duets and monologues for competition. Many of our authors' works have been widely produced at high schools and middle schools, youth theatres and other TYA companies, both amateur and professional, as well as at elementary schools, camps, churches and other institutions serving young audiences and/or actors worldwide. Most are intended for performance by young people, while some are intended for adult actors performing for young audiences.

YouthPLAYS was co-founded by professional playwrights Jonathan Dorf and Ed Shockley. It began merely as an additional outlet to market their own works, which included a substantial body of award-winning published and unpublished plays and musicals. Those interested in their published plays were directed to the respective publishers' websites, and unpublished plays were made available in electronic form. But when they saw the desperate need for material for young actors and audiences—coupled with their experience that numerous quality plays for young people weren't finding a home—they made the decision to represent the work of other playwrights as well. Dozens and dozens of authors are now members of the YouthPLAYS family, with scripts available both electronically and in traditional acting editions. We continue to grow as we look for exciting and challenging plays and musicals for young actors and audiences.

About ProduceaPlay.com

Let's put up a play! Great idea! But producing a play takes time, energy and knowledge. While finding the necessary time and energy is up to you, ProduceaPlay.com is a website designed to assist you with that third element: knowledge.

Created by YouthPLAYS' co-founders, Jonathan Dorf and Ed Shockley, ProduceaPlay.com serves as a resource for producers at all levels as it addresses the many facets of production. As Dorf and Shockley speak from their years of experience (as playwrights, producers, directors and more), they are joined by a group of award-winning theatre professionals and experienced teachers from the world of academic theatre, all making their expertise available for free in the hope of helping this and future generations of producers, whether it's at the school or university level, or in community or professional theatres.

The site is organized into a series of major topics, each of which has its own page that delves into the subject in detail, offering suggestions and links for further information. For example, Publicity covers everything from Publicizing Auditions to How to Use Social Media to Posters to whether it's worth hiring a publicist. Casting details Where to Find the Actors, How to Evaluate a Resume, Callbacks and even Dealing with Problem Actors. You'll find guidance on your Production Timeline, The Theater Space, Picking a Play, Budget, Contracts, Rehearsing the Play, The Program, House Management, Backstage, and many other important subjects.

The site is constantly under construction, so visit often for the latest insights on play producing, and let it help make your play production dreams a reality.

More from YouthPLAYS

Tantrum on the Tracks by Judy Freed (book) and
Marianne Kallen (music and lyrics)
Musical. 45 minutes. 2 males, 2 females, 1 either.

It's a special day for two young train cars: their very first day
with the big train. Dash is so excited he can barely stand still.
But Starlight wishes she were at home with her mom. Can
Engine keep the train together and on track? Or will a temper
tantrum derail everyone's plans in this interactive musical?

***Robin Hood and the Heroes of Sherwood
Forest*** by Randy Wyatt
Adventure. 60-70 minutes. 9-30 males, 6-24 females (18-40+
performers possible).

This fresh adaptation of the classic English tale emphasizes a
community of heroes as Robin Hood and his friends band
together to save the people of Nottingham from unjust taxation
and poverty at the hands of Prince John and his longsuffering
yet cruel Sheriff. Two gypsy orphans, Maid Marion's
handmaiden and a mysterious stranger share a secret that
could win the day—or see Robin hanged by morning!

The Absurdist Super Hero Fairytale by Deanna
Alisa Ableser
Comedy. 30-45 minutes. 5-7 males, 4-6 females, 1 either
(10-12 performers possible).

Basiltown is in jeopardy, and its distracted and overly social
Hero is off having iced Americanos with his fire-breathing pet
dinosaur Fido. With a socially inept Villain on the loose, an
Understudy Narrator in charge, and a ditzy but dreamy Damsel
in distress, can Basiltown's citizens pull together to save their
beloved town while still pursuing their individualized hopes and
dreams?

Telling William Tell by Evan Guilford-Blake
Dramedy. 80-85 minutes. 7-11 males, 4-10 females (11-21 performers possible).

The children grab the spotlight in this retelling of the story of the mythical Swiss hero—famed for shooting an apple off his son's head—framed by a fictionalized story of Rossini writing his famed opera. Music by the great composer enriches this thrilling tale of Switzerland's fight for freedom and the birth of a new work of musical art.

Aesop Refabled by Nicole B. Adkins, Jeff Goode, Adam Hahn, Samantha Macher, Liz Shannon Miller, Dominic Mishler, Mike Rothschild and Dave Ulrich
Comedy. 45-60 minutes. 3-11 males, 3-11 females (3-21 performers possible).

One of L.A.'s edgiest theatre companies brings a modern spin to Aesop's classic yarns, as eight timeless fables get a 21st century reboot. Cupcake bullies, tween warriors, scheming cheerleaders and apocalyptic yellow butterfly people... Each tale takes an unexpected twist in this innovative offering!

Camp Monster by Sharyn Rothstein (book and lyrics) and Kris Kukul (music)
Musical. 60-75 minutes. 7-11 males, 8-11 females (15-22 performers possible).

For years, the sons and daughters of the world's most famous monsters (Dracula, The Wicked Witch, Wolfman, and more) have spent their summer at Camp Flonster, the only camp in the world where young monsters can be themselves. But this year, Camp Flonster has a new director, the diabolical Roseanne Finicula, who harbors a secret desire to rid the world of all monsters! When the young monsters learn of Roseanne's plot, they must put aside their daily squabbles to work together and beat Roseanne at her own game—and keep the world safe for even the strangest among us.

Harry's Hotter at Twilight by Jonathan Dorf

Comedy. 90-100 minutes. 5-25+ males, 7-25+ females (12-50+ performers possible).

In this crazed mash-up parody of *Harry Potter* and *Twilight*—with cameos crashing in from *Lord of the Rings*, *Star Wars*, *Alice in Wonderland* and many other places—you'll encounter deli-owning vegetarians, invisible rabbits, magical carrot weapons, random lunatics, soothing offstage voices, evil gourmets and much more, as everyone's favorite wizards, vampires and werewolves battle to save miserable, gloomy Spork—and indeed the world—from certain destruction.

Sidekickin' It! by Adam J. Goldberg

Comedy. 23-30 minutes. 2 females, 6-9 either (8-11 performers possible).

The story of Robin, a precocious girl with gumption beyond her years, and Daybreak, a superhero who finds he will need more than the ability to lift really, really heavy stuff if he is going to stop humanity's destruction at the hands of the diabolical Von Darkness. Watch Robin teach Daybreak that no power is greater than the power of friendship.

A Stranger on the Bus by Ed Shockley

Drama. About 120 minutes. Flexible cast of 12-50.

The audience experiences the landmark Swann v. Board of Education case that completed the integration of American schools through the dream of a young African-American girl injured in a public school riot. With Jim Crow appearing in the guise of a giant trickster bird to battle the forces of progress, this award-winning epic begins at World War II and journeys to the moment when two innocent children can sit side by side en route to a new era in our nation's history.

Made in the USA
Middletown, DE
28 October 2022

13689284R00056